Sister Maria Celeste's Letters to Her Father, Galileo

Sister Maria Celeste's
Letters to Her Father, Galileo

Edited, Translated, with an
Introduction and Notes
by
Rinaldina Russell

Writers Club Press
San Jose New York Lincoln Shanghai

Sister Maria Celeste's Letters
to Her Father, Galileo

Writers Club Press
an imprint of iUniverse.com, Inc.

For information address:
iUniverse.com, Inc.
5220 S 16th, Ste. 200
Lincoln, NE 68512
www.iuniverse.com

ISBN: 0-595-16279-7

Printed in the United States of America

To the Memory of My Husband, Robert.

Acknowledgements

Many years ago, I came across Sister Maria Celeste's letters to her father, Galileo, and I was impressed by the vividness and immediacy with which they brought back to life a distant Italian world. I began to translate the letters before 1995, working in my spare time and pouring into them much interest and love. Now I rejoice at being given an opportunity to make my translation available to many readers and hope that Maria Celeste's words will come as alive to them as they were to me in the original. My thanks go to Natalie Bacon, who supervised the publication of this book and to Jude Grant, who went through my manuscript with her fine American hand.

Contents

Introduction

The author of the letters presented in this volume was born out of wedlock to Galileo Galilei and to Marina Gamba of Venice on August 13, 1600. At the time of her birth, Galileo was teaching at the University of Padua, and Marina was settled in a house near his residence. The newborn was their first child and was named Virginia, after Galileo's older sister. A second daughter, born one year later, was named after his younger sister Livia, and a baby boy, born in 1606, was christened after his paternal grandfather, Vincenzo Galilei. After their parents separated and Galileo decided to return to Florence, one by one the children were taken from their mother with her consent, never seen by her again. Documentary sources and family letters tell us that Virginia was brought to Florence around 1609 by Galileo's mother, Giulia Ammannati, that in 1613 both Virginia and Livia were accepted as novices by the Franciscan convent of San Matteo at Arcetri near Florence, and that there they took the veil at age fourteen. Virginia pronounced her vows on October 4, 1616, and became a Franciscan nun with the name of Sister Maria Celeste. Suffering from frequent illness, and paying little attention to her ailments, Maria Celeste spent her short life within the enclosure of San Matteo, where she occasionally received visits from relatives and family acquaintances. Except for a few allusions to her in her father's private papers, all we know about her cloistered life comes from the extant 124 notes and letters that she sent to him from May 1623 to December 1633. A few months after the end of the correspondence, in March 1634, Celeste fell ill. In a few weeks, a severe dysentery overtook her, and she died on April 2, 1634.

By the time Virginia entered San Matteo, the custom for young women to join a religious community, either forcibly or by free choice, was well entrenched in Italian society. The ever-increasing cost of marital dowries had long been a serious threat to the financial resources of middle and upper-class families, and the confinement of unwanted daughters into nunneries had become the accepted way of settling their future without curtailing familial assets. As a result of the Italian economic recession at the end of the sixteenth century, the number of religious institutions had increased a hundredfold. At the same time, many instances of unruly conduct in convents had led the Counter Reformation church to establish a stricter set of rules on those entering religious life, but the power of the families, backed by local secular authorities, often prevailed over regulations. Above all, so high was the esteem in which church and society held celibacy, and especially a life of isolation and renunciation for women, that the vocation of the novices and the good intention of their families was not seriously questioned.

Shortly after his arrival in Florence in 1610, Galileo began to look for a permanent home in which to settle both his daughters. As Giulia, the grandmother, was not a woman to be counted on— judging from the portrait left of her in the family correspondence, she was an intolerant, interfering and quarrelsome person—the solution that occurred to the father was the well-established one of making nuns of them. Convents were forbidden to accept novices before the prescribed age of fourteen. As shown in a letter written to him by Alessandro Sertini on March 17, 1610, Galileo tried to find a way around regulations by turning to his connections in the church bureaucracy. In two letters, dated November 18 and December 16, 1611, Cardinal Francesco Maria del Monte emphatically explained to him that placing daughters in a convent before the prescribed time with the view of making nuns of them was not allowed and that Florentine monastic regulations specifically barred sisters from living in the same institution. Even so, both little girls, aged thirteen and twelve, entered San Marco together and took the veil at the minimum required age.

✳   ✳   ✳

By the time Sister Maria Celeste took up her pen in 1613 to write the first letter in this collection, letter writing in Italy had long been a habit among literate people, both as a practical necessity and as a literary pursuit. The best-known letters written by women to family members and to political or business correspondents are those penned by Alessandra Macinghi Strozzi (1406–1471) and by Lucrezia Tornabuoni (1425–1482). At about the same time, the Latin epistle was rediscovered by many humanist scholars and began to be cultivated as a genre. Among the few women who pursued humanistic studies, Laura Cereta (1469–1499) and Cassandra Fedele (1465–1558) are the writers of Latin epistles who most readily come to mind. When, in 1538, Pietro Aretino published a book of his letters in the Italian language, many were ready to follow his example and publishers were quick to provide a very receptive public with collectaneous volumes of correspondence by literary and high society people. Vittoria Colonna was the first woman to have her own collection of letters printed in 1544, and she was imitated by Veronica Franco in 1580 and by Chiara Matraini in 1595. Well before the end of the century, letter writing in Italian had become one of the most successful staples of the printing industry.

The letters made available to a relatively wide public by the press or by private circulation were composed on established epistolographic models. Their intent was generally to present an idealized view of the writer, as befitted a widespread ideal of intellectual and moral composure. Conversely, the letters written to serve an immediate practical need had no literary pretensions and kept a simple tripartite structural form, consisting of the opening, the body of the letter, and the closing salutation. Sister Maria Celeste's letters fall within the latter category. Some of them are short notes accompanying deliveries of food or household items. Many of the longer ones were written in haste and late at night, after an exhausting day, when sleep was overtaking the writer. Even so, and perhaps because of their close adherence to the circumstances of her life, these letters allows us to come into immediate contact with Maria Celeste's world and establish an empathy with it far more readily than do most epistolary collections.

Since medieval times, religious women represented a high percentage of literacy compared with the general female population. They also produced a considerable number and variety of texts. These were either lives of nuns, offering their sisters models of saintly behavior, or chronicles of convents that recorded routine and extraordinary events: the intent of both genres was to enhance the prestige of the order to which the writers belonged. Several religious women wrote mystical works. The best known among them are Angela da Foligno (*Memorial*, 1292–1296), Caterina da Siena (*Dialogue of Divine Providence*, 1377–1378), Caterina da Bologna (*Seven Spiritual Weapons*, 1475), Eustochia da Messina (*Book of Passion*, end of fifteenth century), Felice Rusponi (*Discourse on the Knowledge of God*, 1570; *Dialogue on the Excellence of the Monastic Condition*, 1572), and Maddalena dei Pazzi (*Forty Days,* 1584; *Colloquies,* 1584–1585; *Revelation and Intelligences,* 1585). Caterina da Siena (1347–1380) and Maddalena dei Pazzi (1566–1604) also wrote letters to political and religious authorities and other members of their communities. A most unusual nun was Arcangela Tarabotti (1604–1652) who pursued a prolific and at times worldly literary activity, authored two feminist tracts (*Antisatire,* 1644, and *Whether women are of the same species as men,* 1651), and two works on forced monachation (*Simplicity Deceived* and *Convent Hell*), both published posthumously in 1654 and 1990. Other cloistered women wrote plays that were produced within their monasteries, for an audience of religious people, visiting relatives, and friends. No texts written in convents, or by anyone outside of them, give the reader as valuable a view as Sister Maria Celeste does of the day-to-day life going on inside conventual enclosure, with its problems, pressures, and hardships, as well as its comforts and atmosphere of sheltered intimacy.

❋   ❋   ❋

When Galileo's daughters became two of its residents, San Matteo was, in its economic structure and labor system, in no way different from most Franciscan institutions. The nuns produced the necessary staples by farming the plot of land belonging to the house; at the same time, they were expected to bring in revenue by doing needlework or by the sale of apothecary products. Maria Celeste worked as apothecary and confectioner, and we may infer that her medical preparations were sold to the public, together with those delicacies that she so lovingly prepared when destined for her father. In her letters we also read that the nuns in position of responsibility were personally liable for the budget they managed during their term

xvi   Sister Maria Celeste's Letters to Her Father, Galileo

of office. For this reasons the sisters picked for the positions of greater responsibility were those who came from families thought to be reliable in case of financial default.

Many, however, were the families that could not be counted on, and their cloistered relatives must have felt their abandonment very sharply when, in case of disease especially, they were compelled to fall on their own resources. From Sister Maria Celeste's reports, we gather that illness was an assiduous visitor at San Matteo. And we might be inclined to assume that malnutrition was a factor in it, considering the poor quality of the food provided by the convent. It is not possible to ascertain, however, if the incidents of disease were higher here than what might have been the norm for the population at large, for there are no records of one or the other. What we know with certainty is that the plague of 1630–1633 did not touch the convent, thanks mostly to the enclosure and to the extraordinary measures taken by the religious authorities. In Sister Maria Celeste's running report on the epidemic, we find details of symptoms, of people being taken to isolated hospitals or quarantined in their homes, and of casualties, as they occurred in different social classes. The picture we get of a nephew of Galileo's, with his two surviving children locked up within the walls of their house, has an immediacy and vividness that surpasses for stark effect Alessandro Manzoni's famed portrait of a mother and her dead little daughter in plague-stricken Milan.

With her letter to Galileo of December 10, 1623, Sister Maria Celeste included a memorandum meant to be read by the religious authorities in Rome. It describes how matters stood regarding the confessors' visits to San Matteo and gives a judicious account of the disciplinary situation at the convent and of the spiritual deprivations imposed on the residents that were more religiously inclined. Certainly, not all nuns had their mind on the attainment of spiritual perfection, for we read that several friendships were formed between the sisters and their confessors. The reader might wonder how much influence on the distracted behavior of these women could be attributed to their less than enthusiastic acceptance of a cloistered existence. The lack of perceptive and disinterested guidance, however, was deeply felt by the more religious sisters, and great must have been the humiliation of the intelligent ones among them at being subjected to men of inferior caliber. The neglect was partly due to the history of the convent. Founded as an Augustinian monastery in 1233, San Matteo had been reorganized as a convent of Saint Clare in 1391 by request of the sisters, but it remained under the supervision of the local bishop rather than under the jurisdiction of the Franciscan order. As Sister Maria Celeste explains, the members of the secular clergy assigned to San Matteo by the bishop proved to be less capable and responsible in the performance of their duties than the men of regular religious orders.

The uncommon juridical situation at San Matteo also explains why its rule was not as severe as those observed in Franciscan convents. The letters show, for instance, that the conventual enclosure was not rigidly enforced and that contact with the outside world, either for social or practical purposes, was routinely maintained. If the nuns were prohibited to go out of the convent by the cloistral regulations, there was obviously no prohibition for anyone to enter, except in exceptional cases, as at the time of epidemics. Maria Celeste and other sisters received many visits, from their relatives and from family friends. The convent parlor was a place of social exchange and entertainment for all of them. Dinners were set up there, even at the nuns' table, when Galileo was the visitor. Judging from the ease with which Sister Maria Celeste complies with the request made by the wife of the Florentine ambassador in Rome to come for a visit and see a comedy staged by the nuns, we may assume that San Matteo was one of the many convents where performances were attended by a mixed public of religious and nonreligious visitors.

Regardless of what might have been the nuns' deprivations and compensations, the convent provided its residents with the greatest of all necessities: the possibility of a constant and permanent interpersonal support. The very appellation of "sisters" for the younger nuns, of "mothers" for the older ones, and of "grandmothers" for the very old, gives a clue to the intended, though sublimated, relationships that the convent was meant to establish. These relationships could grow into warm affections, and this is what happened to Sister Maria Celeste, who in the sisters of San Matteo found the emotional support and the close warmth that her relatives did not supply.

※   ※   ※

In 1623 Galileo had been living in Florence for thirteen years. He had arrived from the University of Padua in 1610 to become chief mathematician and philosopher to the grand duke Cosimo II de' Medici. Soon after his arrival, he was embroiled in a complex scientific controversy that would ultimately lead to his trial in Rome—where Sister Maria Celeste addressed the letters in the second part of this collection. His discovery of the Jupiter's satellites had dealt a severe blow to the theory of the earth as the center of the universe, arousing strong objections in many Aristotelian scientists and philosophers, while gaining the approval of the major scientific authorities of the time. Johannes Kepler confirmed Galileo's discoveries publicly in 1611, and, in the same year, Galileo was ceremoniously welcomed in Rome by Christopher Clavius, chief mathematician of the Jesuit Collegio Romano (now the Gregorian University). On that occasion he was received by Pope Paul V and was also introduced to Federico Cesi, one of the most influential personages of the Roman world, who made him a member of the academy he had founded: the Accademia dei Lincei (academy of the lynx-eyed), the first association of the kind to be dedicated to philosophy and science.

The *Letters on the Sunspots* (written in 1613) were the first of Galileo's publications to link his astronomical observations to the geokinetic theory, but the full endorsement of the Copernican system is contained in a letter, widely circulated in learned quarters, that he wrote in December 1613 to his follower and former pupil Benedetto Castelli. In this letter Galileo discusses the purview of science and religion. Both nature and scriptures, he maintains, proceed from God, but while the scriptures must adapt themselves to the intelligence of ordinary people and use a simpleminded language comprehensible to them, nature never deviates from its laws and can be described with precision and coherence in mathematical terms, which only experts understand. With this distinction Galileo may have thought of harmonizing church dogma with the new scientific method, while firmly establishing the unimpeachable authority of scriptures in matters of faith. In fact, though, he was advancing a claim for the reciprocal autonomy of religion and science, which was unwelcome to Roman theologians, especially to the most conservative among them, who were very concerned about discipline and orthodoxy and, to Galieo's misfortune, were perhaps not as conversant as he was with the Tridentine teaching on the interpretation of scriptures. The Italian academic community, who had already considered the new scientific method harmful to philosophy, at this time allied itself to those members of the clergy who thought the Copernican theory to be contrary to religion. In 1614 two Dominican friars began to attack Galileo from the pulpit of their Florentine churches, and, furthermore, one of them, Niccolò Lorini, sent a copy of Galileo's letter to the Holy Office denouncing Galileo and his followers as suspect of heresy.

At that time Aristotelianism, as adapted to Christian thought by Thomas Aquinas, was accepted by the theologians as the foundation of Catholic doctrine. It is therefore understandable that the Dominicans, whose specific task was to track down all suspicions of heresy, would have been the fiercest adversaries of Galileo, for his work undermined the metaphysics of Thomas Aquinas and thereby the orthodoxy of the church. The attitude of the Jesuit scientists of the Roman College had been somewhat different. As much as the task of the order was to place all new scientific discoveries under the aegis of orthodoxy, at the start they honored Galileo's achievements and thus seemed to him to be leaning toward Copernicanism. However, when they became certain that its conciliation with religious dogmas was impossible, the Jesuit fathers adhered to the astronomical system of Tycho Brahe, whose theory, although at variance with the teaching of Aristotle, assumed the immobility of Earth and was in harmony with Thomistic metaphysics. Furthermore, in 1618 Galileo managed to alienate to Collegio Romano in an open controversy, by attacking Orazio Grassi, a member of the college, who in a recent publication had made official the Jesuits' endorsement of Brahe.

At the end of 1616 Galileo went to Rome to defend his views and to clear his name with the Holy Office. This decision was taken against the better judgment of the Florentine ambassador to Rome. The ambassador's advice turned out to be correct, for the pressure that Galileo exercised on some members of the Roman bureaucracy made all of them realize, perhaps for the first time, that the Copernican system infringed upon the astronomy and the metaphysics traditionally taught by the church. The theologians could see what Galileo apparently did not: that distinguishing between the language of the Bible and the language of science meant to undermine the very basis of faith, because it held the superiority of science to all discursive procedures that, like those promoted by religion, attributed the truth to ideas that cannot be demonstrated. On February 24, 1616, the theory that Earth moves and the Sun stands motionless at the center of the universe was officially condemned, and Galileo was enjoined to abandon it by Cardinal Robert Bellarmine, representative of the Holy Office and chief theologian of the Roman College. This unfavorable turn of events, however, did not discouraged the scientist, who persevered in his attempt at persuasion. His amazing moral strength in face of adversity was due to his conviction that the Copernican theory would eventually triumph and the church authorities and Italian studies would suffer grievously from not accepting it. This he explained in a letter to Elia Diodati, dated January 15, 1633.

In 1623, at the time of the first letter to him by his daughter, Galileo was busy completing *The Assayer*. In this text, against the old conception of science founded on established authorities, Galileo proposes a new scientific method, which starts from the direct observation of phenomena, posits a hypothetical model, verifies it through experimentation, and proceeds to infer general laws. The book is rightly considered a masterpiece of cultural propaganda, as well as the logical completion of what was proposed in the letter to Castelli: while in that letter Galileo had defended the independence of science from religious authority, in this book he goes on to claims its autonomy from the scientific establishment. *The Assayer* was published the same year and became a topic of discussion and prognostication in all intellectual circles.

❋   ❋   ❋

These well-known events in Galileo's life, which are either explicitly referred to in the letters or are mentally inferred by the reader, constitute the emotional backbone of Sister Maria Celeste's correspondence. As I have said, many of the letters are short and deal exclusively with domestic transactions, such as exchange of food, the purchase of cloth and thread, the repairing of household objects, and the accounting of expenses and requests for money. Although this may seem mundane, it is in these letters, as much as in the lengthier and more confidential ones, that the dynamics of Sister Maria Celeste's relationship to her father, and of her father to her, is revealed. In the whole, the description of life in the convent and around it, the allusions to Galileo's activities and habits, and the reports of what is being done in his home when he is away in Rome and at Siena, draw a riveting landscape of human situations and emotions. Against this familial and neighborly backdrop, a drama of cross-purposes develops: those of Galileo, ready to wager his future on the approval of the religious authorities, of the Roman clergy, determined to uphold the letter of the Catholic dogma; and of Sister Maria Celeste, unwittingly pinning her reason for living on her father's prestige and her love of him.

Thirteen of Sister Maria Celeste's 124 extant letters are from 1623, 8 in all from 1624 to 1627, 13 again from 1628, 6 from the following year, and 17 and 18 from 1630 and 1631 respectively. Since they were almost all sent to Galileo when he was in Florence, these seventy-five letters can be said to constitute the first part of the collection.

At the beginning of their correspondence, father and daughter are far apart, their lives and interests pertaining to two distant spheres of concern. Galileo had undoubtedly seen the convent as a way of not adding to his financial problems, which were many and mostly of his own making: an expensive lifestyle to begin with and financial obligations, which an excess of family pride made him contract with his relatives, especially his brothers-in-law, and which could not sufficiently be provided for by his stipend and by the sale of his mechanical instruments. Even so, there are signs that he sincerely considered the life of the cloister a way of securing for women in general the avoidance of all life's afflictions and for his daughters in particular, a peaceful and sheltered existence. For in 1600, when he failed to persuade his sister Livia to make permanent her stay in the convent of San Giuliano where she had been sent for an education, he reluctantly accepted her wish, as he put it, "to try the miseries of this world."

In these letters, Sister Maria Celeste never voices an opinion on the subject of her taking the veil; even so, the reality of her father's attitude toward her and her sister could not have escaped her. On several occasions she mournfully refers to the convent as her "prison" and we wonder what she really thought of her own destiny, in whose determination she obviously had no say. What she does say to her father is that she is putting up with each new hardship by piling it together with the many other afflictions she has long learned to accept and live with. For this nun, the adaptation to the convent enclosure went together with the observance of its regulations, as shown by her memorandum of October 10, 1623, but she does not seem to me to have had a genuinely religious vocation, as some scholars concluded, who were struck by her patient resignation and goodwill. She rather seems to share the ways of perceiving and thinking that were typical of the milieu that nurtured her since childhood. Maria Celeste is confident that trust in God will guide humankind through all calamities, and she repeatedly counts human tribulations as pluses for the afterlife. In one letter she voices the Catholic belief that faith and good works will save people's souls, and, in a few cases, she seems to be prone to popular superstitions, as when she expresses the hope in the waters blessed by a holy woman, or in the therapeutic powers of the image of the Virgin being carried out in procession during the outbreak of the plague.

From the start Maria Celeste shows great eagerness to know more about her father's world and makes requests to that effect that are almost obsequious. Galileo's mind, on the other hand, is far from San Matteo and its problems. In 1624 he began to write the *Dialogue on the Two Chief Systems of the World* and embarked himself in what would prove to be a fateful campaign of publicity for the Copernican system. The letters written to him in this period lead us to assume that he was then looking for familial affection in the direction of his brother's family and his newly married son, Vincenzo. In 1627 Michelangelo's wife and most of their numerous children arrived from Munich to live with him. Vincenzo graduated from the University of Pisa in the spring of 1628; in the fall Galileo entered negotiations for his son's marriage to Sestilia Bocchineri. These events rebound on the gentle nun, who is soon taken up with the thought of meeting the new bride and preparing a gift for her. Galileo's cohabitation with his brother's family does not prove a happy one and in 1628 Michelangelo recalls his brood back to Bavaria, reproaching his brother for not providing sufficiently for them. Vincenzo marries in January 1629, and his brother-in-law, Geri Bocchineri, who is the private secretary of the grand duke Ferdinand II, becomes an attentive and concerned member of the Galilei family and a frequent appearance in Sister Maria Celeste's correspondence. In the fall of the same year, a baby boy is born to Vincenzo and Sestilia and is named after his grandfather. He is referred to by his aunt as Galileino—translated from the Italian as "small Galileo"—and is described as having the temperament as well as the name of his namesake.

As Galileo's relationship with his live-in relatives becomes strained, his awareness of his elder daughter's qualities increases. Provided with no other training than the reading and writing taught in the convent—Galileo reserved a formal education and a university training for his son, who was also the only child to be legitimatized—Maria Celeste can nonetheless rely on her natural intelligence and talents and on a disposition to apply her mind to a variety of activities and tasks. This daughter is also considerate and tactful. She suppresses all jealousy for those who live close to her beloved father; she befriends the people who take care of him and whom he loves; she consoles him when he has been offended and when he grieves for the death of his dear ones. Thus slowly, almost surreptitiously, she takes up a solid place in his heart.

On her side, Sister Maria Celeste is unaware of displacing her craving for emotional outlet on her father, and she repeatedly brings up the subject of her feelings toward him, explaining them in terms of filial devotion. With the passing of time her emotional involvement with him has intensified. She alternatively laments his absence and thanks him for his quick responses to her calls. She prepares for him many delicacies and in turn receives a great quantity of comestibles not only for her sister, Sister Arcangela, and herself but also for several sick nuns whom she looks after. Uppermost in her mind is Galileo himself, his health and his activities. As he seems too deeply immersed in his studies, she lectures him on the necessity of giving one's body a rest. When he loses his appetite and feels sluggish, she prepares an appetizing restorative for him. As her demands on him grow in frequency, his readiness to attend to her needs strengthens her dependency on him. She is gratified by his successes and basks in his special attention to her. These compensatory rewards of self-esteem and satisfied pride, rather than discouraged, were most likely reinforced by the convent community.

Of the letters written in this first period, only two were mailed to Rome. One is dated April 26, 1624, and reaches Galileo while journeying to the Vatican. The other letter is dated May 15, 1630. The reason for the second trip was to solicit permission to publish the *Dialogue,* the book completed earlier in the year. At about the same time, the plague breaks out in the countryside near Florence and Galileo's assistant suddenly dies of it. Vincenzo runs away in fear of the contagion and leaves his child and his father alone at Bellosguardo. By this time, father and daughter have developed a strong reciprocal bond. He provides for all her needs and wishes; she sends him restoratives and preservatives against the plague, of a physical as well as a spiritual character. Slowly, not only does her attitude towards him become more self-assured and motherly, but she often urges him to come to live at Arcetri, impressing upon him that the move will save him the discomfort of riding up the hill to the convent all the way from Bellosguardo. A house, called Il Gioiello, is offered for rent by one Esaù Martellini for thirty-five scudi a year. Galileo moves into it in the fall of 1631, and the correspondence come to a halt.

We do not know what happens to Sister Maria Celeste and to the other sisters in the convent in this while, but are very well acquainted with the dramatic events pertaining to the publication of the *Dialogue.* Niccolò Riccardi, the Jesuit father in charge of printing permits at the Sacred Palace in Rome, had given hints that Galileo's book would be allowed to discuss the Copernican theory if presented as a pure mathematical hypothesis. To that effect a preface written by Riccardi himself reaches Florence in July 1631, together with further instructions about the conclusion of the book. The volume comes out of the press in February 1632, Galileo quickly sends thirty-two copies to Bologna and one to Rome, to Cardinal Francesco Barberini, the pope's nephew. A few months later, to the apparent surprise of the author, an order is given to halt the printing of the book. Toward the end of summer Galileo is called to Rome to stand trial before the Holy Office. The grand duke's protestations and several medical certificates attesting to Galileo's poor state of health are to no avail, and, after many delays, he is told by Ferdinand II to obey the pontiff.

In January 1633 Galileo leaves his home, and in February Sister Maria Celeste's correspondence with him resumes. The forty-nine letters remaining in this collection were sent to Galileo when, from February to July 1633, he is again in Rome, this time to answer allegations of heresy, and when, from July to December, he is at Siena, detained in the palace of the local archbishop, Ascanio Piccolomini. These letters are lengthier, richer in details and in drama.

While Galileo's destiny is being decided in Rome and his social position in Florence is at risk, his need for emotional support increases and Maria Celeste does the utmost to supply it. Conversely, she grows in strength and stature, extending her sphere of action to his household—relatives and servants—and among his supporters. In her telling, many characters, although briefly sketched, stand out. First of all, Piera, Galileo's housekeeper, with her industry, common sense, and a sympathetic attachment to the family. Then the young and devoted servant Geppo, who has several misadventures: with friends of the family, who require his services; with a master repairman, who refuses to return Galileo's clock; in the hospital, where he goes to cure his liver and is infected with rabies. Not to be forgotten are the antics of Galileo's mule, finicky with her feed and wary of carrying anyone but her master. There are characters that impress us for their tactfulness and gentlemanly behavior: Geri Boçchineri, Francesco Rondinelli, Doctor Ronconi. And there are many minor figures that are removed from the major scene of events but are charmingly alive: the nun who sends friendly messages to Galileo; the organist who asks for a piece of music that can be played on the convent organ, which has several keys missing; the nun who goes into a fit when she is reminded of her relatives' neglect of her; the eighty-year-old Sister Giulia, who is critically ill and is about to be given extreme unction, but surprisingly recovers to live and exchange courtly compliments with Galileo and do some good dunking in the archbishop's wine.

All throughout there are moments of intense beauty: Piera's scales of desire; Maria Celeste's exposition on the tripartite love uniting her to her father and to Luisa; the rose in winter that she sends to Galileo, whose thorns will remind him of Christ's suffering on the cross and whose green leaves are a symbol of "the brightness and joy of eternal spring in heaven"; and, of course, the consolatory letter that Maria Celeste sends to her father upon learning of the Holy Office condemnation of him and his work.

Maria Celeste's main duties in the convent are those of dispenser and confectioner. Later on she is given the added duties of convent letter writer and director of the choir. During her father's absence, she takes constant care of the sick and the dying. Among her charges is a spirited young nun, reputed to have been the most beautiful Florentine girl in the last three hundred years, now slowly dying of consumption. Sister Maria Celeste is none too well herself, continuously suffering from debilitating headaches and tremendous tooth pains. She is furthermore affected by a persistent intestinal blockage. She patiently accepts this and many other inconveniences, some of which are caused by her none too considerate sibling. Sister Arcangela, Galileo's younger daughter, comes out in all her selfish nature, inefficiency, fondness of comforts and rare foods, in her continuous need of attention, with apparently no thought for Maria Celeste's sacrifices in her favor. Lately, during her term of office as convent steward, she runs into considerable debts, thus adding to Maria Celeste's worries.

Fortunately for the latter, the lack of sisterly love and support is compensated by the congenial friendship of Sister Luisa, who is endowed with the same generosity of spirit as herself and with the same passion for the preparation of medical prescriptions and delicacies. Maria Celeste can also count on the support of a group of special friends among the younger nuns who gather together to sew and chat and whose greetings she adds to her own in closing her letters to Galileo. To such a group, we may infer, Maria Celeste confides some details of what she knows of her famous father, deriving from it a pleasure of pride and reflected glory, whose sudden disappearance, upon his condemnation, must have made her grief and dismay perilously difficult to bear.

In his letters from Rome, Galileo tries to lessen the negative effect that his trial might have among relatives and supporters. For the benefit of all possible readers at home, he writes to Maria Celeste that things are looking up at the papal curia. Special attention is taken at first that Sister Maria Celeste be told as little as possible about the terrible events overtaking him. Her excited reaction at one of his optimistic announcements shows the extent of her apprehension. The other sisters are aware of her feelings, and they too are overjoyed when the news of Galileo's move to Siena arrives. The scene with the nuns crying for happiness and running toward Maria Celeste to rejoice with her is one of the most moving moments in the collection. Ultimately, notwithstanding Galileo's tactful strategy, Sister Maria Celeste can no longer be sheltered from the effects of her father's condemnation. When she writes to him after learning of the final sentence, we feel how great must have been the effort to repress her own despair, to muster the courage needed to offer him encouragement and comfort. It is Sister Maria Celeste's apprehension, her reactions to Galileo's silence and to the rumors and behavior of people around her that create the suspense and the emotional crescendo building up the drama in the second part of the collection. The closure comes suddenly and unexpectedly with the news that Galileo is about to arrive.

After her father's return to Arcetri, the sense of hopelessness that had slowly penetrated Sister Maria Celeste's spirit during his trial must have prevailed in the end, thus becoming a contributing factor in her untimely death in 1634. The correctness of this assumption is proved by what Galieo himself wrote in a letter sent to Elia Diodati in the summer of the same year: "Her illness, brought about by a host of melancholy humors, gathered together during my absence, which she believed very troubled, soon degenerated into a precipitous dysentery, and she died, aged thirty-three, leaving me in the greatest misery."

❧   ❧   ❧

Sister Maria Celeste's original letters are contained in the thirteenth section of Part I of the collection of Galileo's papers, as they are now organized and preserved in Raccolta Palatina 23, of the Biblioteca Nazionale Centrale in Florence, Italy. Galileo's responses to these letters were never found. They were presumably lost when many of his manuscripts were destroyed, or in the convent of San Matteo itself, or perhaps they have been simply misplaced in what remains in the provincial archives since the closure of the convent. His daughter's letters were kept by Galileo among his other correspondence and at his death fell into the hands of his pupil Vincenzo Viviani. We owe the present collection to Battista Clementi de' Nelli, who at the end of the eighteenth century bought them from the heirs of Viviani, who thoughtlessly had allowed a great number of Galileo's papers to be dispersed or destroyed. Several nineteenth-century scholars published a number of letters or excerpts from them. Antonio Favaro edited the first complete edition in 1891, and, in a long introductory essay mainly about Galileo, assembled all is known about the daughter and other members of the family. While appreciating the intelligence and piety of Sister Maria Celeste, scholars have looked at her becoming Galileo's strongest support later in his life as her main praiseworthy trait. Favaro lauded her for her "merits of mind and heart," for having comforted the old man—for whom she supposedly felt "a child-like admiration"—and for having looked after him with motherly tenderness. Almost unchanged is the judgment that Antonio Banfi gave of Maria Celeste in his 1961 essay where the young nun is defined by her intense spirituality and a forgiving empathy for the scientist that was nourished by an innate maternal instinct.[1]

I have based my translation on Favaro's edition, and I have compared it with the original manuscripts at the library of Florence as well as with the edition prepared by Francesco Saverio and Maria Rossi and with the Genova edition of 1992. In my translation I have tried to render the tone, the level of familiarity and literacy of the original text, and in order to achieve a comparable English style, I thought best to break down Sister Maria Celeste's long and complex sentences into a few shorter ones. All changes have been made in order to remain faithful to the spirit of Maria Celeste's letters and to make their multiple references clear. I hope this translation will allow the reader an appreciative insight into the real character of a memorable seventeenth-century woman and provide an illuminating glimpse into the ordinary and extraordinary lives of many people who chanced to witness one of the most important events in the intellectual history of humankind.

※　　　　　※　　　　　※

Letters to Her Father, Galileo

I

[Sent to Florence]

To our most illustrious and most beloved Lord and Father:

We were heartbroken at the news of the death of your dear sister and dear aunt of ours.[2] We feel a great sorrow, I say, not only for her passing, but also because we know how grieved Your Lordship must be for this loss, which is for you, one might say, greater than any other could be, for you held no one else as dear. So we can guess how severe this sudden blow must be for you.

As I said, we too share a great part of your grief, although we ought to draw sufficient solace from the consideration of all human misery and from knowing that we are all here on earth as visitors and passersby, who will soon depart for our true abode in heaven, where perfect happiness resides and where, we can hope, that blessed soul has gone. So we urge you to take comfort, for the love of God, and place yourself in his hands, who, as you know well, would be displeased, should you do otherwise. Besides, you would cause harm to yourself and to us, and we cannot help feeling very downcast whenever we hear that you are in distress and out of sorts, for we have no one else in the world but you.

I will say no more, except that we pray God from the bottom of our hearts that he may comfort you and be with you always. We greet you affectionately.

Your most devoted and affectionate daughter, Sister Maria Celeste.

From San Matteo. May 10, 1623.

II

[Sent to the villa][3]

To the most illustrious Lord and Father:

It is impossible to describe the delight Your Lordship gave me in letting me read the letters you received from that renowned cardinal, now pope, for I could well see how great is the affection he has for you and how high is the esteem in which he holds your talent.[4] I have read and reread the letters with special pleasure, and now I am sending them back to you as you requested. I showed them to no one but Sister Arcangela, who too was overjoyed in reading how favored Your Lordship is by so influential a person. May it please God to grant you as much good health as you need to satisfy your wish of paying His Holiness a visit, and enjoy greater favors to come. Besides, reading of the many promises he made in his letters, we may well hope that some help could easily be obtained for our brother as well. Meanwhile we shall pray God, who is the source of all blessing, to grant you the fulfillment of your desires, if that is truly for the best.

I expect that on this occasion Your Lordship will have written a very beautiful letter to His Holiness to congratulate him on his new high office, and I would be grateful if it might please you to let me see a copy, for I am rather curious about it. I thank you to no end for the letters that you have already sent, and also for the melons, which were indeed very welcome. I am writing in great haste, so please excuse me for putting all this down so badly. My usual friends join me in sending you the warmest greetings.

Most devoted daughter Sister Maria Celeste
August 10, [1623].[5]

III

[Sent to the villa]

To the most illustrious Lord and Father:

Your very loving letter made me fully realize how scanty my sagacity was in thinking that Your Lordship would write so soon to such a personage or, I should say, to the most sublime man in the whole world. I thank you for your warning, and I am certain that your love for me will make allowances for my great ignorance, as well as for many other faults that are to be found in me. I wish I could be warned and reprimanded by you for all my shortcomings, for I would gratefully acquire that understanding and discernment that is missing in me.

Since your protracted indisposition prevents us from seeing you even once in a while, we must patiently submit to the will of God, who makes everything happen for our best. What I do is this: I put away all Your Lordship's letters in a safe place, and, when I am not busy, I read them again and again with the utmost pleasure. So you can imagine how pleased I am to read those you received from people so virtuous and so well disposed toward you. As I do not want to tire you any further, I will close this note by sending you affectionate greetings, together with those of Sister Arcangela, Sister Diamante, and all the others who are here with me.

Most devoted daughter Sister Maria Celeste
August 13, 1623.

IV

[Sent to Florence]

To the most illustrious Lord and Father:

I have heard from our bailiff that Your Lordship has taken ill in Florence.[6] As it seems quite unusual for you to leave your home while suffering from your customary aches and pains, I feel rather apprehensive about it and go on thinking that your condition must be more serious than usual.

So please tell the bailiff how you really are so that in case you are not as ill as we fear, he may bring us his reassurances. In truth, I never am so fully aware of being a cloistered nun as when I am told that you are ill, because then I would want to come to you and take care of you with all the diligence of which I am capable. All the same, may the Lord be thanked for everything, because without his willing so, not a single leaf would turn. In any event, I expect you to have all you need, but if there is anything we could do, let us know and we will serve you as best as we can. In the meanwhile, as our usual, we shall pray the Lord for your good health, and that he may bestow his grace on you. Finally, we greet you from the bottom of our hearts, joined in this by all the other nuns here.

Most devoted daughter Sister Maria Celeste
From San Matteo. August 17, 1623.

V

[Sent to Florence]

To the most illustrious and most beloved Lord and Father:

Being most anxious to have news of Your Lordship, I am sending our bailiff with the excuse of bringing these fish-shaped cakes made of marzipan, which, if not as delectable as the fish out of Arno, will not be, I do not think, totally unpalatable to you, especially coming as they do from San Matteo. I do not wish to distract you or give you annoyance by requesting a written answer; it would suffice for me to hear from the bailiff's mouth how you are, and whether we can be of any service to you. Sister Chiara[7] warmly commends herself to her father and brother and also to Your Lordship. And so do we both, while wishing and praying our Lord for your perfect health.

Most devoted daughter Sister Maria Celeste
From San Matteo. August 21, 1623.

We have received the cantaloupes and the watermelons. They were very good and we thank you for them.

VI

[Sent to Florence]

Most illustrious Lord and Father:

We were very sorry to hear from Sir Benedetto[8] that not only Your Lordship's health is not improving but that, besides, you are in bed with great pains and no appetite. Even so, we firmly hope that in his mercy the Lord will soon grant you some measure of strength, if not total fitness. It seems almost impossible that it should not be so, for you seem capable of tolerating your many persistent troubles with a great deal of patience, which, no doubt, will merit greater glory for you in your next life.

I have managed to find a few plums for you, and here they are, though not as perfect as I wish them to be. So, please, take into account my good intention.

I would like to remind you that when you receive a letter from those gentlemen in Rome, you promised to let me see it. I will not mention the other letters that you told me you would be sending, for I suppose you left them at the villa. I do not wish to tire you any further, so I close here and send my heartfelt greetings, together with those of Sister Arcangela and the usual nuns. May our Lord give you good cheer and be with you always.

Most devoted daughter Sister Maria Celeste Galilei
From San Matteo. August 28, 1623.

VII

[Sent to Florence]

To the most illustrious and most beloved Lord and Father:

It was with the greatest pleasure that I read the beautiful letters you sent me. I thank you and return them to you in the hope of seeing others in the future. I am also sending a letter for Vincenzo, with prayer of your forwarding it to him at your convenience. I congratulate you on your recovery and give thanks to God for it. Please, continue to take good care of yourself until you are completely recovered. I am grateful to you for your many kindnesses: really, I do not want you to take so much trouble for us, in the condition you are in now. Many affectionate greetings, on the part of Sister Arcangela as well, and may our God grant you an abundance of grace.

Most devoted daughter Sister Maria Celeste
From San Matteo. The last day of August, 1623.

VIII

[Sent to Florence]

To the most revered Lord and Father:

Here is the letter I copied for you. I hope it is to your satisfaction so that you may continue to avail yourself of my work, because being busy in Your Lordship's service is my greatest pleasure and contentment.

Mother Superior[9] is not in a position to buy wine until the small quantity we made ourselves has run out. She sends her apologies for not being able to please you, and thanks you for your advice in this matter. The wine you had delivered to us for Sister Arcangela is indeed excellent, and she sends her thanks. Moreover, she and I thank you for the thread,[10] and for all your other gifts.

Lest I delay the servant, I shall say nothing else, except for sending you warm greetings on the part of all of us here, and we pray our Lord God for the fulfillment of all your desires.

Your devoted daughter Sister Maria Celeste
From San Matteo, on the last day of September.

IX

[Sent to the villa at Bellosguardo]

To the most beloved Lord and Father:

The fruit that Your Lordship sent us was very welcome, especially because it is Lent for us now. As appreciated was the caviar you had someone deliver for Sister Arcangela. We both thank you.

Vincenzo has a great shortage of collars, although he pays no attention to the matter and usually asks for one to be starched only when he is in great need of it. But we find it very difficult to mend the ones he has—they are far too old—and we would like to make four new ones for him, trimmed with lace and with matching cuffs. Having neither time nor money, I would very much like Your Lordship to supply me with what is needed: a yard of cambric linen and at least eighteen or twenty lire, with which to buy lace from Signora Ortensia, who does wonderful work. Mind you, this item of clothing takes a lot of garnish, for the fashion nowadays calls for very large collars. And since Vincenzo has been lately so very obedient to Your Lordship, who always wears cuffs, I dare say he now deserves to have some beautiful ones himself. So don't be surprised if I ask for so much money.

I shall say no more, except that I greet you both with all my heart, on the part of sister Arcangela as well. May the Lord keep you safe.

Most devoted Sister Maria Celeste
[1623]

X

[Sent to the villa]

Most beloved Lord and Father:

Here are the other shirts we made for you, and also your over-all, which I mended the best way I could. I am also returning the letters you sent for me to read: they are all so beautiful that they have increased my desire to read many more. At the moment I am working on the napkins, so I would like you to send the fringes that are to be sewn at the end. Please keep in mind that they should be very wide, for the napkins are rather short.

I have placed Sister Arcangela in the hands of the doctor once more to see, with God's help, whether she may be cured of that bothersome infirmity of hers, which causes me endless anxiety.

Salvatore[11] told us that Your Lordship intends to come to see us soon. We greatly yearn for this visit. But remember the promise you made of spending the evening here. You will be allowed to dine with us in the parlor, because the excommunication is addressed to the tablecloth, not to the people around it.[12]

Enclosed is a paper that not only will tell you what our needs are but also will give you reason to laugh at my silly writing. Even so, knowing the great benevolence with which Your Lordship always praises my scarce talent has given me the courage to go on with it. So excuse me and come to my aid with your customary kindness. I thank you for the fish and send affectionate salutations together with Sister Arcangela's.

Most devoted daughter Sister Maria Celeste
From San Matteo. October 20, 1623.

XI

[Sent to the villa]

Most illustrious and most revered Lord and Father:

If I wanted to say in words how beholden we are for the gift Your Lordship sent us, not only I would fail to express our deep appreciation for it, but I believe you would not be very pleased, because, in your benevolence, you would have our gratitude rather than verbal demonstrations or ceremonies. We therefore must thank you in the best way we know, and that is by praying for you, and so recognizing and compensating for this act of kindness and for numberless others, and by far greater favors we have already received from you.

When I asked you to provide me with ten yards of material, I meant a quality with a narrow width and not one so wide, so beautiful and expensive. This will certainly be more than ample for the shirts.

I let you imagine how great my pleasure is in reading the letters that Your Lordship has been sending all along. Just considering how kind it is of you to let me know about them and have me share with you the many courtesies you receive from these gentlemen is by itself sufficient to fill me with happiness, even though I find it hard to accept the news that you will soon start on a journey, for I shall be left without you.[13] And I keep imagining that you will be gone for a long time, nor do I think I am wrong. Your Lordship may well believe me, for I am saying the truth when I declare that, besides you, there is no one else in the world who could give me any degree of happiness. I will nonetheless make no complaint about your departure, because this would mean regretting something that is much to your liking. So I rejoice for it and pray the Lord, now and always, to bestow upon you grace and perfect health so that you might start on this voyage in all prosperity and afterward return to us greatly satisfied with its outcome, and live happily for many years thereafter. And I hope it will come to pass, with God's help.

Although your thoughtfulness makes it unnecessary, I recommend our poor brother to you, and pray you may excuse him on account of his youth, for that is what led him to commit his error, which deserves forgiveness, being his first.[14] So again I entreat you to take him with you to Rome, for in that city occasions will not be lacking to offer him the support that fatherly obligation, love, and your natural benevolence demand.

Not wishing to become tiresome, I will close this letter by commending myself to your grace and reminding you of a visit promised to us a long time ago. Sister Arcangela and the others here join me in sending endless greetings.

Most devoted daughter Sister Maria Celeste Galilei
From San Matteo. October 29, 1623.

XII

[Sent to Bellosguardo]

To the most illustrious and beloved Lord and Father:

The inexhaustible love I feel for Your Lordship and the fear that this sudden snap of cold weather, usually so harmful to you, may cause a recrudescence of your usual infirmity and of other complaints no longer allow me to remain without news of you. I am therefore sending this note to learn something about your present state of health and also when you plan to start on your journey. I have hurried the work on the napkins and now they are almost finished. In sewing the fringes on, however, I found that for some of them I am short of the necessary material, of which here is a sample, and that is about one yard of it. I would be very grateful if you could let me have it right away so that I can hand over the whole lot before you leave. This is the reason I hurried the work so much.

As I do not have a room of my own to sleep in, Sister Diamante kindly allows me to spend the night in her bedroom, thus depriving her own sister of it for my sake. But this winter the weather is so harsh, and my head always so congested, that I do not know how long I can resist there, unless you come to my rescue. I would like to borrow some of your bed curtains: a set of the white ones that you are not using at the moment would do very well. I would really like knowing if you could do me this favor. In addition, I

19

would greatly appreciate your letting me have that book of yours that is just off the press, for great is my wish to see and read it.[15]

I made these pastries a few days ago with the intention of giving them to you during your good-bye visit. But as your departure will not be as soon as I had feared, I am sending them before they become stale. Sister Arcangela is still under doctor's supervision and feels none too well, with two cauteries applied to her thighs. I am not quite recovered myself as yet, but I am so accustomed to poor health that I take little notice of it, as I see furthermore that it is God's will always to visit me with some kind of trouble or another. I thank him nonetheless for everything, and pray him to grant to Your Lordship the height of the greatest joy. And finally I send you my greetings together with those of Sister Arcangela.

Most devoted daughter Sister Maria Celeste
From San Matteo. November 21, 1623.

If there are any collars you wish to have cleaned, please send them.

XIII

[Sent to Bellosguardo]

To the most illustrious and most beloved Lord and Father:

I had hoped to reply in person to what Your Lordship said in that most kind letter of several days ago, but, since the bad weather prevents me from doing so, I decided to put down my ideas in writing. The great benevolence with which you propose to help our convent gives me great joy. I conferred with Mother Superior and with some of the older sisters. They showed the gratitude that the nature of your proposal deserves. But as they could not decide what choice to make, Mother Superior wrote to our governor asking for his opinion. He replied that considering the immediate needs of our convent, it would seem wiser to solicit a contribution in money. In the meanwhile I discussed the matter over with a nun whose judgment and goodness surpass any other sister's, motivated as she is by good zeal rather than by emotion or personal interest. She advises me—in fact, she begs me—to ask something that undoubtedly would be very useful to the convent and easy for Your Lordship to obtain: that is, the authorization from the Holy Father to have as confessor a regular—or a friar, we can say—on condition of changing him every three years, as it is done in other convents.[16] By this I do not mean that we should be exempted from our current rule but only that we ought to be able to receive from the confessor the Holy Sacraments. I cannot impress upon you strongly enough how beneficial this would be for us, and for very many reasons, some of which I have listed in the enclosed paper.

I do not expect Your Lordship to act on this matter on a mere word of mine. You may want to consult some experienced person, or you might try, when you are here, to throw a feeler in order to find out what Mother Superior and some of the senior nuns have in mind, without revealing the reason for inquiring. And I beg you not to mention it to Sir Benedetto, for he unquestionably would tell Sister Chiara, and she in turn would tell the whole convent. In that case we would be finished, because with so many brains at work, it would be impossible not to be faced with different opinions, and anyone hostile to the idea would have the chance to interpose some obstacle in the way of our plan. On consideration, it does not seem fair to me, for the sake of one or two nuns, to deprive all the others of a common benefit, both temporal and spiritual, that might derive from such a change. This said, we wish to comply with your judgment. What remains to be done now is for Your Lordship to judiciously consider whether it may be admissible to ask for such authorization and in which way we might go about it to obtain it more easily, for to me it seems a very legitimate request, the more so for being urgently needed.

I am writing to you today because, the weather being so beautiful, you might want to come to see us before it changes, so I wish to inform you about the task you would have to go about here with the old nuns, as I have just explained.

Lest I become too much of a nuisance, I'll stop writing and leave out many things until I can discuss them with you in person. Today we are waiting for the vicar general to arrive for the election of the new abbess. May it please God to have the nun elected who more conforms to his will. And may he grant you his holy grace in great abundance.

Most devoted daughter Sister Maria Celeste
From San Matteo. December 10, 1623.

Memorandum
The foremost reason that drives me to make such request is
that I know and see how the little knowledge and experience
these priests have of the rules and obligations of us nuns, and
this situation gives us occasion, I should say license, to live
more and more freely, and with little observance of our rule.
And who is to deny that by living with little fear of God we are
not also to bring continuous material misery upon ourselves?
We therefore must remove the first cause of our offense, which
is what I just said.

The second reason is that the convent, being as poor as you
know it is, cannot satisfy the claims of the confessors, by paying
them the salary due to them when they leave, every three years.
I happen to know that with the excuse of the money we still
owe them, three of our past confessors often come here to dine
and are in the habit of getting very friendly with some of the
nuns; and, what is worse, they talk and complain about us
everywhere they go, thus making us the laughing stock of all
Casentino—which is the region our confessors usually come
from—for these men are more accustomed to hunting hares
than to guiding the souls of religious women. Your Lordship my
believe me when I say that, should I describe the blunders of
our present confessor, I would never come to an end, for they
are infinite and incredible.

Third, a regular friar will never be so ignorant as not to
know far more than any of these men, or, if he is that ignorant,
he certainly will not, for every small problem of ours, go asking
for advise, at the bishop's palace or elsewhere, on what his deci-

sion and behavior ought to be, as these priests do all day long.
He will instead query some experienced father of his own order,
so our problems will be known only in one monastery and not
all around Florence, as it happens now. Furthermore, a regular
friar is more likely to know, if nothing else by experience, how
he is supposed to behave with nuns so that we may live as quietly as possible, while a priest, who comes here with no knowledge of monastic life, will reach the end of his term without
ever learning the rules and regulations of our house.

We do not ask for a man of any specific order, and submit to
the judgment of those who will advance our request and obtain
the authorization for the change. I must say, however, that the
friars of Santa Maria Maggiore, who were here many times as
substitute confessors, gave us great satisfaction; and I believe
they would do to our case more than anyone else: first, for
being fathers very observant of the rule and held in good opinion by all; and, second, being used to living in poverty, they
would not exact great rewards from us, nor would they care to
be offered a pleasurable welcome, as men of other orders
demanded when they came here, or as the priests who are sent
to us as our confessors customarily do, who, serving the convent only for three years, think of nothing else in that time
except of their personal and material interest, and the more
they manage to get out of us, the cleverer they consider themselves to be.

But without my expanding on more possible reasons, Your
Lordship can inquire in what condition the convent of San Jacopo
and Santa Monaca operated, and others too, and how well they have
been doing since they began to be governed by friars who knew how
to lead them back to the good path. This does not mean that we wish
to abandon the observance of our rule, but only that we want to

receive the sacraments and would like to be governed by experienced men, with a measure of good education.[17]

XIV

[Sent to Rome][18]

Most illustrious and most beloved Lord and Father:

The news we received (together with the letter that Your Lordship ordered to be delivered to Sir Benedetto), that you have comfortably reached Acquasparta, pleased us tremendously and we thank the Holy Lord for it. We are also happy to learn how graciously Prince Cesi has received you[19] and are confident that the occasion will come to rejoice even more upon hearing about your arrival in Rome, where you are expected by some very important people. Even so, all your successes are counterbalanced, I am certain, by the great pain caused you by the sudden death of Signor Virginio Cesarini,[20] a man you esteemed and loved so much. This sad announcement has disturbed me a great deal, and so has the thought of your losing such a dear friend, the more so because you expected to be reunited with him at the earliest. No doubt this event gives us reasons to reflect on the uncertainty and vanity of all the hopes we entertain in this ugly world of ours.

Lest I go on sermonizing too long, I will add nothing else, except for giving Your Lordship news of ourselves—we are very well indeed—and sending you affectionate greeting in name of all the nuns as well. And I pray our Lord to grant you the fulfillment of all your just desires.

Most devoted daughter Sister Maria Celeste
From San Matteo. April 26, 1624.

XV

[Sent to the villa at Bellosguardo]

To the most illustrious and most revered Lord and Father:

Of the candied citrons you ordered, I have prepared only as many as I am delivering to you at present, because, being the citrons past their time, I was afraid they would not turn out as well as I wished—and in truth they have not. With the citrons, I am letting you have two comfit pears for the coming days of fasting. But to add a little more to the gift, I am sending you a rose, which will certainly please you, being such an extraordinary thing at this time of the year. And the more so because, with the rose, you will be able to accept the thorns, which represent the cruel suffering of our Lord the Savior, while the green leaves symbolize the hope that we may entertain (thanks to our Lord's Passion) that one day, after the brief and dark winter of our present life, we shall be able to reach the brightness and the joy of eternal spring in heaven. May God grant it to us in his mercy.

I'll come to the end of this note now, and greet you very affectionately, together with Sister Arcangela. We both remain with the wish to learn something about Your Lordship's present state of health.

Most devoted daughter Sister Maria Celeste
From San Matteo. December 19, 1625.

I am sending back the tablecloth in which the lamb came wrapped. You still have a pillowcase of ours—which we sent with the shirts—a basket and a bedspread.

XVI

[Sent to Bellosguardo]

Most beloved Lord and Father:

As I do not know how to thank you for your many acts of kindness, I can only say that I shall pray God to reward you with accrued grace; and may he allow you to spend the upcoming holiday season very joyfully indeed, this year and for many years to come. And may he grant the same to our Vincenzo, for whom I am sending herewith two collars and two pairs of new cuffs. The little time I can dispose of did not allow me to make the decorations myself, so I would like him to excuse me if the collars are not to his complete satisfaction. I will not fail to make him others with lacework, as I promised. Sister Arcangela is feeling much better, but she remains in bed. Her confessor is due at this moment, so I will not delay. Please enjoy these marzipan cakes at supper this evening. I commend myself to both of you with all my heart.

Your most devoted daughter Sister Maria Celeste
[Before Christmas 1624][21]

XVII

[Sent to Bellosguardo]

To the most illustrious and most beloved Lord and Father:

Your Lordship's neglect in paying us a visit (with the weather being very mild now and, from what I understand, you in good health and, furthermore, free of the obligation to attend the court[22]) would be sufficient reason for me to fear that the great love you always showed toward us might be diminishing. But your frequent demonstrations of affection toward us have abated my apprehension. So I am rather inclined to assume that you may be postponing your visit because of the scanty pleasure you get in coming here, both from us, who are, I should say, too inept to satisfy you completely, and from the others who fail to do so, for whatever reason it may be.

Consequently, I will stop complaining and pretend to have no qualms whatsoever, but I beg you to conform by coming to see us, if not entirely to your wishes, at least to our desire: which is to be with you all the time, if that were possible, and pay you those respects that your merit and our debt towards you would require. And because this is not allowed, we shall not be amiss in satisfying our obligation by offering our prayers to God that he may grant you his grace in this life and eternal happiness in the next.

I am afraid Vincenzo will complain about us. We are so late with the collars he asked for, although he has great need for them, as he told us. Will Your Lordship please send us a small quantity of the cambric linen we need in order to finish this work for him, and let us also have some news of him, as we would like it so. If you need to have anything done, which may keep us busy, please say so; and remember that serving you is our greatest pleasure. In closing, I commend myself to you, together with Sister Arcangela.

Most devoted daughter Sister Maria Celeste
From San Matteo. On the first day of Lent, 1626.[23]

XVIII

[Sent to Florence]

Most beloved Lord and Father:

I shall gladly candy your citrons in the way most pleasing to your taste. For the preparation of both the syrup and the morsels, two pounds of sugar will probably be necessary, and, if you prefer them made with good musket wine, I would greatly appreciate your sending what is needed, because I find myself totally out of money. And in case you want me to candy some rosemary flowers as well, the way you always enjoy so much, send a larger quantity of sugar. We have not received our platter; and you still have the carafe and a white dish.

I would not want you to worry exceedingly about us. Take care of yourself, and if you return to the villa, refrain from working in the garden until the weather improves, because this habit of yours has been very harmful to your health. Being in a great hurry I shall stop writing here and send you my heartfelt regards. May the Lord bestow his grace upon you.

I hope to receive the sugar at the earliest; otherwise the citrons will perish. I should also be grateful if, by chance, you can get hold of a few more. I have something in mind that I will tell you about when you come here, for I long to see you presently.

Your most devoted daughter Sister Maria Celeste
[Lent 1626]

XIX

[Sent to Bellosguardo]

Most beloved Lord and Father:

We thank Your Lordship for the many lovely gifts. We will enjoy them for the love of you. The rosemary flowers you sent I reckon will fill four jars, and since they are very damp, we shall wait for the others you say will arrive, for ordinarily we begin to prepare them as they start to whither. At the moment I am working on the citrons I received a short while ago. I think they will come out better than the last ones.

I wish you a very happy Easter, this year and in many years to come. I commend myself to you, and the same does Sister Arcangela.

Your most affectionate daughter Sister Maria Celeste
[Lent 1626]

XX

[Sent to Bellosguardo]

Most beloved Lord and Father:

It was a great pleasure for me to learn the other day that Your Lordship is well, which I cannot say of myself, having been in bed with some temperature since Sunday. The fever would have been something to worry about, says the doctor, if a mild case of diarrhea had not cut down its vigor and reduced it considerably. Since God grants me the good fortune of preserving Your Lordship in good health, I shall take advantage of this possibility and I shall turn to you for everything I need, with the confidence fostered in me by your increasing love and kindness. Especially now, when I must take fairly good care of myself and try to bring some relief to my extreme debility, I would be grateful if Your Lordship could send me some money. I need many things, but they are too numerous to enumerate and almost impossible for you to remember. I can only say that the provisions supplied by the convent consist of some very coarse bread, bad-quality beef, and wine that is about to turn to vinegar. I am now savoring the wine you sent to me, of which I still have a flask and a half. For the time being I do not need any more, because I drink very little. I usually share it with the other sisters, as I ought to, especially with Sister Luisa. She greatly enjoyed your last flask, which was rather light, in color that is, but strong in character. If in your coop there is a hen that no longer lays eggs, it would make good condensed soup for me, as the doctor suggests. In the meanwhile I am sending you twelve slices of cake, for I don't dispose of anything else. Enjoy them for the love of me. I send you greetings on the part of all my friends and also of the abbess, who is my very kind friend and so well disposed toward me. May our Lord keep you healthy.

Your most devoted daughter Sister Maria Celeste
[Lent 1627]

XXI

[Sent to Bellosguardo]

To the most illustrious and most beloved Lord and Father:

These few lines of verse will tell you of my feelings toward you at this Christmastime. I desire for you the fulfillment of all your aspirations in this and in many seasons to come, and pray the Lord to let you enjoy the holy festivities in utmost tranquillity. I wish the same for the rest of the family. Here are also a few little things for uncle's children: the largest collar with the handcuffs is for Albertino, the other two are for his younger brothers, the little dog for the girl, the pastries for everybody, except for the aniseed cakes, which are for Your Lordship.[24] Please consider my good intention, which would be ready to do much more.

I received the wine and the rhubarb too, and I thank you. I pray the Lord to reward you for your gracious generosity with an increase of his holy grace. And, finally, I commend myself affectionately to all.

Your most devoted daughter Sister Maria Celeste
From San Matteo. On Christmas Eve 1627.

XXII

[Sent to Bellosguardo]

Most beloved Lord and Father:

I truly believe that a father's love can wear out as a result of the objectionable habits and the bad conduct of his children. This belief is confirmed by some signs Your Lordship has given us, which make it appear that the cordial affection that you once felt toward us has in some way waned. You have not paid us a visit for more than three months now, which to us seem like three years, and, although you are in good health, you have not sent us a line of writing for quite a long while.

I have thoroughly examined my conduct to see if, on my part, I did anything to deserve such punishment, and I found that, although involuntarily, I behaved toward you carelessly, or rather thoughtlessly, and without the solicitude that is required by my obligation to write to you with some frequency. This, together with, alas, many other unquestionable deficiencies on my part, was enough to promote my fears. Nonetheless, my failure is to be attributed to a lack of strength rather than to one of will, for my continuous ill health has kept me away from all activities, whatever they might have been. For more than a month now, I have been suffering from very strong headaches, with no relief either by day or night. However, just now the pain has diminished somewhat, God be thanked, and I have immediately picked up my pen to write this lament, which, coming as it does in the carnival sea-son, ought to be taken in jest. Provided you will remember our wish to see you as soon as the weather will allow it. Meanwhile, I am sending these few confections that I received as a gift. They must be quite hard by now, for I have been saving them for some time, in the expectation of handing them to you when you came. The ring cakes are for Anna Maria and her little brothers. I am also enclosing a letter for Vincenzo in the hope it will remind him of our existence. I am afraid he has forgotten us, for he never writes a line. We send greetings to you and to aunt, from the bot-tom of our heart, and I pray God for your true happiness.

Your most devoted daughter Sister Maria Celeste
From San Matteo. March 4, 1628.

XXIII

[Sent to Florence]

Most beloved Lord and Father:

As I could not think of anything you might like to have, I considered that perhaps I would please you more if I sent something for Signora Barbara[25] and the other women who are taking care of you. To them I feel very obliged, for the love of you. So here are a few pastries for you all to enjoy during this season of Lent. If you were to ask for something that could really pleasure you, we would be immensely gratified, for our greatest wish is to be useful to you in any small way we can.

Yesterday I had a tooth extracted which had been giving me a great deal of discomfort. Now I am free of the pain that has tortured me for the last two months, although my head is not quite normal yet. I expect in a short time I shall recover completely, as I hope and if it pleases God, whom I pray to bestow perfect health on you. And in closing I send greetings to you, to Vincenzo, to aunt, and to everybody in the family, on the part of Sister Arcangela as well.

Most devoted daughter Sister Maria Celeste
From San Matteo. March 18, 1628.

XXIV

[Sent to Santo Spirito][26]

Most beloved Lord and Father:

Here is the cinnamon water, which I think will not be quite to your liking, having been made so recently. If you are out of distilled water, you could return the carafe to the bailiff, so I could send you some more. Tell me if you enjoyed the cooked pear and whether I should prepare you another, although pears being out of season are not at this time as good as they will be later on. I send greetings to aunt and to all of you but Vincenzo, for I don't know if he has already left.[27] I would like very much to be informed. Please be in good cheer so that you may recover more speedily and come to see us soon, for you have promised and we greatly long for it. Let us know if you need anything. May our Lord grant you his holy grace.

Most devoted daughter Sister Maria Celeste
From San Matteo. March 22, 1628.

XXV

[Sent to Florence]

Most beloved Lord and Father:

Since it is impossible for me to attend to you in person, as I very much would want to do (this impossibility alone makes this conventual enclosure hard for me to bear), I keep you constantly in my thoughts and, at the same time, I would like to have news of you daily. Since the bailiff could not see you the other day, I am sending him again today with the excuse of taking these two bits of candied citron to you. You could also tell him if you require anything from us, and whether the quince pear was to your liking and whether I should prepare you another one. Now I stop writing, lest I become too tiresome. I commend myself to your affection and always pray our Lord for your complete recovery. The same do Sister Arcangela and my other friends here.

Your devoted daughter Sister Maria Celeste
March 24, 1628.

XXVI

[Sent to Florence]

Most beloved Lord and Father:

The joy we feel in hearing about your speedy recovery is without bounds, and most gratefully I thank the Lord, who is the giver of all things. In order not to disobey your kind command to give you news of us, I shall tell you that on doctor's orders I am not observing Lent. And since I have become toothless well before old age, I would like to have some mutton, preferably fat, although I eat little of that too. Sister Arcangela would be happy to have some little thing for her to eat at supper; she would especially enjoy some white wine. I am telling you this because I do not wish to go against your orders. I feel really embarrassed that you should take so much trouble for us while you are still ailing. I do not know what to say, except that you are a father, and a very loving one, in whom, after God, we place all our trust. May it please the Lord to keep you safe for us much longer, if it is for your good. And in closing now, I commend myself to you from the bottom of my heart.

Your devoted daughter Sister Maria Celeste
From San Matteo. March 25, 1628.

XXVII

[Sent to Bellosguardo]

Most beloved Lord and Father:

Today the weather was so pleasant as to give me hope that perhaps I would have the pleasure of seeing you. As you did not arrive, little Alberto's visit was very welcome[28] for he told us that you are well and will soon come to call, together with aunt; but—and this "but" spoils everything—hearing that you have gone back to work in your orchard, as your usual custom, I am worried not a little. What with the weather being still on the cool side and with your not being yet up to strength, I am afraid this activity will be injurious to your well-being. My Lordship, I pray you, do not forget so soon the condition you were in only a short while ago,[29] and, please, have a bit more consideration for your own person than for what is out there in the orchard. As it is, I somehow believe that you dare take such risks less for your love of plants than for the pleasure derived from attending to them. But in Lenten time it beholds to all of us to make some sacrifice. And, in the spirit of Lent, you can make exactly this one, of depriving yourself for a while of this diversion that is so agreeable for you.

The other day I wrote that I would be pleased if by chance you could get hold of a few more citrons. Now I am asking again if you can find a way to procure one or two more for me. It wouldn't matter if they were not from the countryside around here. I would appreciate your doing this favor very much, because Sister Luisa and I plan to prepare a few sweetmeats for Cavalier Marzi, who has just been elected our governor again. He will be here during Holy Week to give us the Easter blessing and we would like to offer him three or four of those morsels he likes so much. The ones I prepared for you are not ready yet, for the weather has not been dry enough, except today.

I am sending a good quantity of raisins and six pine cones for the children. Thank you for the meat. But do not trouble to send any more, because now I am feeling well again and I think I will start observing Lent next Friday. And finally, I send greetings to you and to aunt. May the Holy God favor you.

Yours most devoted daughter Sister Maria Celeste
[Lent 1628]

XXVIII

[Sent to Bellosguardo]

Most beloved Lord and Father:

Both Sister Luisa and I thank you enormously for the citrons. They are very welcome not only because they are coming from you but also because we had no other way of procuring them. The food you sent for Lent was also very appreciated, particularly by Sister Arcangela. As for myself, wishing to keep in reasonably good health, I live under a very strict diet, so you need not fear I might go to excess. And I shall obey you and will not eat the eggs.

I was very happy to get the pictures. When you reply to Mechilde's letter, please thank her for us and return her greetings in duplicate.[30] I am returning the boys' collars. At the bottom of the basket you will find about eight candied pieces. Two we kept for ourselves, as you kindly insisted. I also made some jelly with the citron syrup and with the extra sugar we received, and some more with the rosemary flowers, but the jellies are not set enough to travel.

I am happy for your continued recovery, and I pray our Lord to restore you back to your perfect health, if it is for the best. And in closing I commend myself to you, together with Sister Arcangela and Sister Luisa.

Your most devoted daughter Sister Maria Celeste

April 8, 1628.

And to aunt, of course.

XXIX

[Sent to Florence]

To the most beloved Lord and Father:

Your Lordship's generosity and kindness could not be compared to Papazzoni's stinginess,[31] but rather to Alexander the Great's magnanimity (and I wish your strength as well were equal to his courage). But, really, I would compare Your Lordship to a pelican, because this animal goes to the extreme of ripping his own guts open in order to nourish his offsprings. And in truth, you would not hesitate to deprive yourself of something that is essential to you in order to come to the need of your dear daughters. So how could I be afraid of vexing you by suggesting the idea of sending me two or three pounds of sugar with which I could candy the pears you just let me have? Not for a single moment could I believe that this worrisome thought might cause your heart to quiver! And in this certainty, I delayed answering your note.

Another reason for the delay is that the doctor arrived just as I was about to pick up my pen. I had sent for him on account of my teacher who has been ill for several days. It was therefore impossible to satisfy my obligation to you, for I had to assist her, as well as three more nuns who were also sick, and I could assign no one else to the task. Forgive then my delay, and, I pray you, fill up this flask with some of your wine for the above-mentioned teacher.

Any wine you have will do, as long as it is not too tart, for the doctor has advised against it, and the convent wine is very harsh.

I would like to know if you could get several yards of linen from Pisa for two dear nuns who keep asking for it. If you could arrange it for me, I would send you the sample and the eight scudi[32] that they insisted on paying me with. I shall stop here because I am in a great hurry. I pray the Lord to grant you his holy grace, and I send greetings to you, to aunt and to all the little devils.

Your devoted daughter Sister Maria Celeste
From San Matteo. April 10, 1628.

XXX

[Sent to Bellosguardo]

Most beloved Lord and Father:

The candied citrons have turned out to perfection. I am gratified by the way they look and by the diligent work that goes into
the preparation. But although this activity gives me great pleasure,
I like even better being at your service, for this is what gratifies me
more than anything else.

I am sending you one additional jar of rosemary-flower preserve, made with the sugar left over from the preparation of the
candied fruit. The morsels are not ready yet, neither is the syrup,
which I think is coming out pretty well. As to the quantity of
sugar needed to fill the jars that I am now sending to you, it is at
least six ounces each jar; in fact the one I already sent to you took
almost seven. You can trust me to tell you the right amounts,
although I am averaging—so to speak. I see Your Lordship wants
to pull my leg, for you know well that I do not say lies, especially
in this kind of thing.

In the meanwhile, if you have emptied those three glass beakers
of mine, please send them with the rosemary flowers so that I can
fill them up again. I would also like you to tidy up all around your
house, now that the priest will come for the Easter blessing, and, if
you find some empty vases or cruets that would do for my pharmacy, you can get rid of them by sending them here where they

would come very handy. A few boxes would do too. Well, you know what I mean.

As to the *cantucci*,[33] we will draw up the bill, as you propose, now that Lent is over. Here is some sponge cake for yourself and some pastries for the boys. Thank you for the wine, which I will share with the grandmother[34] and a few friends, for it is not for me, really. I send affectionate greetings to you and to aunt, and pray the Lord to keep you in good health.

Your most devoted daughter Sister Maria Celeste
April 19, 1628.

XXXI

[Sent to Bellosguardo]

Most beloved Lord and Father:

   The weather has been very beautiful in the past few days, but you did not appear, so I must assume that you either are not feeling well or have gone to Pisa. To find out how things stand, I am sending this woman over, and, at the same time, I let you have the candied fruit I prepared for you. The five bits separated from the rest were made with the citrons you sent more recently. I believe they are tastier than the others, both because the citrons were better and fresher and because the sugar was more refined, so they also came out whiter. This was the sugar I got from Sister Luisa, for the one you gave me had run out. I hope you did not forget to send me more rosemary flowers, as you promised in your last letter. I am waiting to receive them any moment now. I am reminding you of it for I do not think they will keep for long. If Your Lordship goes to Pisa before coming to see us, remember to do me the favor I asked you about, to buy the linen, that is. Would you also see, I pray you, if around the house you have a small quantity of woollen material. I would like to make a stomach warmer. Now that our winter clothes are about to be taken away from us, my poor frail stomach will resent the cold terribly.

At the moment I am very busy and will not add anything else to this letter, except for sending you warm greetings. May the Lord bestow on you true happiness.

Your most devoted daughter Sister Maria Celeste
San Matteo. April 28, 1628.

XXXII

[Sent to Bellosguardo]

Most beloved Lord and Father:

As I did not write to you for quite a while, you may have understandably presumed that I had forgotten you, just as I might suspect you of having misled the road to the convent, simply because you last traveled on it a long time ago. But in fact, just as scarcity of time, and not the above reason, is the certain and only reason for my failure to write—for there is not one hour in the day that I can truly call mine—so I must believe that some important business rather than forgetfulness has prevented you from coming to see us.[35] And now that our Vincenzo calls on us instead of you, we may put our minds to rest and forget about your coming, for he can give reliable news of you.

Everything we hear from him pleases us a good deal, except that you have started to go out gardening in the morning again. This worries me no end, for fear that some serious and bothersome infirmity might befall you, just as it happened last winter. So I beg you, try to stop this habit of yours, for it hurts you so. If you do not want to give it up for the sake of your health, do it at least for the love of your children, who want you to reach a decrepit old age; and this will not happen if you carry on with so little caution. I am saying this out of experience, because every time I linger outdoors, my poor head resents it terribly. How much more dangerous it must be for you!

When Vincenzo was here last time, Sister Chiara asked him for eight or ten oranges. Now she addresses her request to you, provided of course your oranges are at a fairly good point of ripeness, for she needs them Monday morning. I am sending back your dish with a cooked pear in it, which I believe you will like, and some sponge cake as well.

If you have collars that need bleaching, you can send them with the other basket of ours and with that bedspread that you still have. Affectionate greetings to you and Vincenzo, the same from Sister Arcangela and all the others here. May God bestow his holy grace on you.

Most devoted daughter Sister Maria Celeste
From San Matteo. On Saint Martin's Day, 1628.

XXXIII

[Sent to Bellosguardo]

To the most beloved Lord and Father:

I should never tire of thanking our blessed Lord, because he never takes pleasure in sending me some trouble without at the same time granting me many satisfactions. Among them, and for me the greatest in the world, is his preserving Your Lordship safe and sound for me. I say, preserving you for me because you are always willing and ready to satisfy every need of mine. Truly, if I did not know of such good disposition, I would hardly risk bothering you so often. To make it short, I will say Sister Arcangela has been ill for more than eight days now, and although at first I did not pay much attention to it, thinking it might be a cold, I later realized that she needed to be bled. Not only has she fallen into the usual despondency, but she is at present afflicted by a general infection as well. Her legs in particular are covered all over with small red boils, which give her such pains that she is hardly able to move. I recognize her need of bloodletting—although this treatment has never done her much good—and for this reason I am waiting for the doctor to arrive this morning. But since no money is assigned to me for an emergency of this kind, I beg you, for God's sake, relieve me of this worry and send some cash. I need it for many more things as well, things that would be too tedious to you to enumerate now. If Vincenzo could spare the time, I would like him to be here. With him I could talk freely about my problems, which must be sent to me for some purpose, coming as they do from God.

Here is a cooked pear for you, one of those beautiful ones you sent to me a short while ago. I have found a new way of preparing pears, which I think you will like better. I would be obliged if you returned the bedspread, because it is not mine. In closing I greet you with love and pray the Lord to keep you well and sound.

Your devoted daughter Sister Maria Celeste
From San Matteo. December 10, 1628.

XXXIV

[Sent to Bellosguardo]

Most beloved Lord and Father:

The sudden and unexpected news that Vincenzo gave of the settlement of his marriage contract—and of so good an alliance!—brought me a joy I cannot express, except by saying that as great is the love I feel for you, so is my pleasure for every happiness you might experience, which on this occasion must be immense.[36] So I offer my congratulations and pray the Lord to preserve you for a very long time so that you may enjoy the satisfaction that the good qualities of your son—and brother of mine—seem to promise. My affection for him grows every day, for I see what a quiet and wise young man he has become.

I would have preferred to congratulate you about this in person, but since it is not possible, I beg you to tell me at least in writing what gift you wish me to send to the future bride. Would it be better to send it to Prato, when Vincenzo is there, or wait for her to come to Florence? This custom of sending gifts to the bride is pecular to us nuns, something moreover she must be well acquainted with, having spent some time in a convent herself. I am therefore waiting for your decision. In the meanwhile, I salute you with all my heart.

Your most devoted daughter Sister Maria Celeste
[Probably written at the end of December 1628]

XXXV

[Sent to Bellosguardo]

Most beloved Lord and Father:

I must presume that you have not been able to come to see us in the last several days because you have been and are terribly busy. So, wishing to hear from you, I resolved to write again to tell you, in reference to the gift for the bride, that I am willing to wait as long as you like, provided you let me know your decision a few days in advance. I shall take advantage of your kind offer of help, because, as perceptive as you are, you can easily judge that with the possibilities I dispose of in my condition, my means are equal neither to my desire nor to my obligations. So I am sending you a list of the most expensive ingredients needed to make a batch of pastries, and I leave the least costly for me to take care of. You can tell me whether you want me to bake other things as well, such as prosciutto scones, or anything like that. The ones we make here would be less expensive than those you can buy from the grocer, and we surely would make them with all possible care.

I would appreciate more than anything your letting me know what gift you would like me to send to the bride, for my wish is no other than to please Your Lordship. My idea is to give her a beautiful apron, because it is something useful and inexpensive. We could sew the apron ourselves, while such things as collars and ruffs, which are fashionable nowadays, would be too difficult for us to make.

Ordinarily I would consider it inappropriate to consult you on such trifling matters as these, but I know that your judgment in small as well as in important things is better than ours. So I will wait for your instructions, and, in closing, I commend myself to you and to Vincenzo, together with Sister Arcangela. May the Lord bless you.

Your most devoted daughter Sister Maria Celeste
From San Matteo. January 4, 1629.

You can give the bailiff the basket in which the collars arrived, together with three things: the dirty overall, one bath towel, and one small cloth.

XXXVI

[Sent to Bellosguardo]

Most beloved Lord and Father:

We were indeed very pleased with the bride. She is so sociable and gracious! But what I was most glad to see was that she has great affection for you, and we imagine she will give such proofs of love to you as we ourselves would like to give, if we were allowed. We shall not fail, nonetheless, to do our own part, by always commending you to God, for we are greatly obliged to you not only as daughters but also as the desolate orphans we would be if you were to be taken from us.

I wish I could express my feelings adequately! I could then be certain that you would have no doubts about my loving you as tenderly as no other daughter has ever loved her father. But I can only say that I love you more than I love myself. And that is because I recognize that after God I owe my being to you, as I owe you so many other innumerable benefits. I am therefore obliged and ready, whenever needed, to expose my life to whatever danger and hardship for you, with the exception of bringing offense to the Divine Majesty.

Pray, forgive me for detaining you so long and so tediously, but at times my love has the best of me. I did not sit down to write with all this in mind, but because I wanted to tell you that if you could return the clock Saturday evening, the sister sacristan, who wakes us up in the morning, would be much obliged. In case you do not get a chance to look at it in such short time, please ignore my request, for it would be better for us to wait a little longer, if need be, in order to have it back repaired.

I would also appreciate knowing if you would be willing to make an exchange with us. Would you take back the theorbo you gave us several years ago, and give us instead a breviary each? The breviaries we received when we became nuns are now totally worn out. These are the instruments we use every day, while the theorbo[37] remains abandoned in the dust and in danger of being damaged every time we are obliged to lend it to someone outside the convent, lest we be discourteous. If you agree to this exchange, let me know when I can send it. And as to the breviaries, we do not care if they are not gilded. We would be happy if they included all the saints that have been canonized recently, and if the printing were clear, because we would be able to use them well into our old age, if we are allowed to reach it.

I wanted to make you some rosemary jelly, but I am waiting for you to return some of my glass jars, for I have nothing to put it in. And if around your house there are any empty pots or bottles not being used, they would be very useful to me in the shop.

Finally, I close and send you heartfelt greetings, together with those of Sister Arcangela and everybody else's here. May God keep you in his grace.

Most devoted daughter Sister Maria Celeste
March 22, 1629.

XXXVII

[Sent to Bellosguardo]

Most beloved Lord and Father:

Your Lordship must have surmised, at least in part, the discomforts I have been suffering, since I entered this convent, because of the scarcity of cells. Now I shall explain the situation more clearly. The small cell for which two or three years ago we paid thirty-six scudi to our teacher (as is the custom here), I was obliged to surrender entirely to Sister Arcangela so that she may be as separate as possible from the above-mentioned nun. Troubled as this nun is by her persistent fits of temper, I was afraid her continuous talk might cause Sister Arcangela no small annoyance. Besides, Sister Arcangela is of a character very different from mine, and herself rather extravagant, so it turns out to be easier for me to give in to her in many matters in order to be able to live with her in that peace and harmony that our mutual affection requires. The result is that I am spending the night in the troublesome company of the said teacher (although I manage very well with God's help, from whom these travails are coming, indubitably for my own good), and during the day I wander about like a pilgrim, because I do not have a place to withdraw to, even for one hour, if I need to. I do not wish to have a big or beautiful room; a tiny one would suffice, such as the very small cell that at present happens to be offered by a nun in need of money. Thanks to Sister Luisa's tactful mediation, this nun prefers me to the others who are trying to buy it from her. But since the cost is of thirty-five scudi, and I have only ten, which Sister Luisa has managed to find for me, plus five I expect to get from my income, I will not be able to take possession of the cell unless you come to my rescue with the difference, which is twenty scudi.

I am presenting my need to you with filial self-assurance and without ceremony, because I do not want to jeopardize your loving disposition toward me, which I had so often occasion to put to the test. I will only add that the necessity I describe above is among the most compelling ones I am experiencing in my present situation, and that you may be certain, loving me as you do and always wishing my happiness, that having a cell of my own would give me great comfort and pleasure. This is a permissible and honest desire, for I wish nothing else but a little quiet and solitude. You perhaps would say that the needed sum being so high, I ought to draw the necessary cash from the amount that the convent still owes you. To which I can answer (and, in any case, it is impossible to draw twenty scudi from it at this time, while the nun who wants to sell is in urgent need of money) that you promised Mother Superior not to ask for a reimbursement unless a chance presents itself to the convent of getting rid of the debt without paying it back in cash. I do not think you would deny me this favor, which I am asking for in God's name, just like one of those people who are in great need and have been thrown into prison. I shouldn't say only "in need" but also "ashamed," because in your presence I would not dare to advance my request so openly, not even to Vincenzo, for that matter. So in all hope I turn to you in writing, knowing that you can and will help me. And in closing, I recommend myself very affectionately to you, and also to Vincenzo and his bride. May the Lord keep you happy forever
    Most devoted daughter Sister Maria Celeste
    From San Matteo. July 8, 1629.

XXXVIII

[Sent to Florence]

Most beloved Lord and Father:

We got back the cruet decorated with the scorpions, and both I and Sister Luisa thank you no end. A few days ago, we thought of sending you some of the cinnamon water we made recently—we think you might enjoy it, with the colder weather coming—but we could find no one to take it to you. If you lived in a house near us—as I would wish—there would be no such problems. Well, we shall wait for the first chance to present itself. In the meanwhile I would be glad to know how well Lisabetta[38] is doing and if she wants anything from us. When you send the cloth for your collars, and the scarf for sister-in-law, I would like you to let me have as a sample an old collar that fits you well and would also appreciate receiving the Brescian thread you promised, because I will use it on the scarf. At this moment I am terribly sleepy and I am going to bed because it is very late. I send you my love, together with Sister Luisa's and Sister Arcangela's; the same to Vincenzo and the bride. May our Lord protect you.

Most devoted daughter Sister Maria Celeste
September 6, 1629.

XXXIX

[Sent to Bellosguardo]

Most beloved Lord and Father:

I am very sorry that you are not well, the more so because you customarily get worse after you have been to see us. I am bold to say that I would willingly give up the pleasure of your visits, as much as I long for them, were I certain that the journey to the convent is harmful to you. But since I believe your indisposition to be really due to the bad weather, I beseech you to take the best possible care of yourself.

Sister Luisa could not have been happier about your taking advantage of our dispensary (though to a very small degree). She is afraid the medicinal syrup she made is not as good as she would like, it being destined for your consumption. We are sending five ounces of it, as you ordered, and we are at your disposal if you need more. Ordinarily, the taste of the mixture is mitigated with a syrup made of citron rind, so we send you some of this too for you to try. If you need anything else, let us know.

Thank you for the cuttings. If you have a few more, I would like to have them. Soon I will send you some little thing for Porzia.[39] Here is some marzipan. Enjoy it for the love of me. Greetings to you, to Vincenzo, and to sister-in-law. I am sorry that she is in bed; if there is anything I can help her with, I will be very pleased to oblige. May our Lord grant you his holy grace.

67

Your most devoted daughter Sister Maria Celeste
November 10, 1629.

XL

[Sent to Bellosguardo]

Most beloved Lord and Father:

Now that the storm of our many troubles has somewhat sub-
sided, I am going to tell you all about it, not only because I wish to
lighten the weight on my mind, but also because I would like to be
excused if once or twice I wrote to you without due consideration
or out of sorts. The fact is that I was almost beside myself with
fright, and so were all the other nuns, on account of our teacher
who, overcome by her humors—furors I should say—in the past
few days has twice attempted to kill herself. The first time she
attempted it by banging her head and face against the floor. She
did it with such fury that her features became monstrously
deformed. The second time she tried by inflicting thirteen wounds
on herself, two in the throat, two in the stomach, and all the others in her bowels. This happened during the night. I can let you
imagine the horror that overcame us all when we found her
reduced to that state and all covered with blood. But what surprised us more is that while she was mangling herself, she shouted
and called us to her room and then asked for a confessor, and,
during the confession, she gave him the knife so that nobody
could see it (although, as far as we can conjecture, it must have
been a penknife). She seemed to be deranged and cunning at the
same time. We can only conclude that these are God's mysterious

doings, for she is still alive when she ought to have died after-wards of natural causes, because her wounds are very deep, according to the surgeon. For this reason we have been watching her day and night. At the moment, all of us are in good health, thank God, while she is tied up in bed, but with the same out-bursts as before; and this situation keeps us in continuous fear of some other extravagance.

After these travails, I wish to mention something else that has been bothering me. A while ago, you kindly gave me the twenty scudi I had entreated you for (when you were here and asked me if I had obtained the cell, I did not dare to tell you what was on my mind), so I went, money in hand, to see the nun who was selling. This nun was in great need of cash and would have gladly accepted the sum I had with me but could not resolve to separate herself from her room, she liked it so much. So, as I wished noth-ing else but enjoy the comfort of that tiny cell, nothing came of it and no agreement was reached. Now, since I told you that I was going to buy the cell and then I did not, I became very worried, not so much for being deprived of it as out of fear that you might think that you had been manipulated: for it seemed that I had told you one thing and then I did another, although that was not my intention. Besides, I was worried because I did not want to hold on to the money. So, when Mother Superior had a sudden need of cash, I was glad to lend her what I had, and later, out of gratitude and love, she promised me the room of the sick nun I told you about, which is large and beautiful, and is worth one hundred twenty scudi. Mother Superior is willing to let me have it for eighty, and in this she goes out of the way to favor me, as she has done in numerous occasions. And because she well knows that I cannot put eighty scudi together, she proposes to accept for this transaction the thirty scudi that the convent has been holding for you for so long, provided of course we have your consent. Of this

I did not think I could doubt, since that arrangement would turn out to my great satisfaction and comfort and, at the same time, would please Your Lordship. I therefore pray to give me an answer, so that I may satisfy Mother Superior who, as her term of office is coming to an end very soon, is in the process of tidying up her accounts.

I would like to know how you are feeling these days that the weather has greatly improved. For lack of anything better, I am sending you a small quantity of quince jam, which was made with apples and flavored with poverty. If you do not like it, perhaps someone else will. As to the sister-in-law, I do not know what to send her, for nothing is to her liking.[40] But in case she does not mind to get something made by nuns, let us know what it is, for we wish to please her. I have not forgotten my obligation to Porzia, but so far I have not been able to do anything about it. In the meanwhile, if you can find the other scraps of material you promised, I would be very pleased to have them now, as I need to use them with those that I already have.

One more thing. While I was writing this letter, the sick nun I mentioned above has had another relapse and we think she might die soon. In which case, I must give the rest of the money to Mother so that she could take care of the funeral expenses.

I have come across the necklace of agates you gave me a while ago. To me it is quite useless while it would do, I think very well, for sister-in-law. I am therefore sending the necklace to you, in the hope that you will have it and in exchange send me a few scudi for this current necessity of mine. Hopefully this money will make up for the rest of the sum I need, so, God willing, I will not be forced to bother you any longer, which is what matters to me most.

The truth is that I do not have anyone else to whom to turn, nor do I want to; I only have you and Sister Luisa, my very faithful friend, who puts herself out for me as much as she can.

Unfortunately, we are both locked in this convent and lack the mobility we would need to take care of ourselves. Blessed be the Lord who never fails to come to our aid, and, for the love of him, I pray you to forgive me if I am such a nuisance and hope that God will not leave unrewarded the many benefits with which you have favored and keep favoring me. So I pray him with all my heart, and, at the same time, I beg you to excuse me if there are mistakes in this letter, because I cannot spare the time to read this tirade over again.

Your devoted daughter Sister Maria Celeste
From San Matteo. November 22, 1629.

XLI

[Sent to Bellosguardo]

Most beloved Lord and Father:

I am afraid that your visit the other day may have caused the usual inconvenience of perhaps worsening your indisposition. I am therefore sending someone to see you in the hope I shall learn not what I fear but what I wish to hear, that is to say, that you are well. I cannot say the same of us. Sister Luisa's teacher—the very one you saw the other day and could not believe to be eighty years old, for she is so very fit—well, the same evening she was suddenly taken ill with cough and fever, and her pains were so terrible as to make us fear she was done for. Sister Luisa naturally is very upset by this, for she loves her much. In addition, Sister Violante has been taken to bed with some temperature and is to remain there, on doctor's orders. According to the same doctor, we may have little hope for her. Yesterday morning she took her medicines and now she is on a strict regime. If Your Lordship were so kind as to send me a flask of well-aged red wine for her, I would be very happy. Unfortunately our wine is acid, and for Sister Violante I wish to do as much as I can until the very end.

I have not forgotten my debt to Porzia, and I am therefore sending these scarves we have made ourselves, and this braid. You may want to give them to her on my part and, at the same time, see if you find other remainders of fine material. Well, do as you think best. And please enjoy these fresh eggs for me tonight. Finally, I commend myself and the rest of us to you, and pray the Lord to keep you in his grace.

Your devoted daughter Sister Maria Celeste
January 14, 1630.

XLII

[Sent to Bellosguardo]

Most beloved Lord and Father:

In answer to your very welcome letter, I'll say that Sister Arcangela is well and I almost well. On Doctor Ronconi's advice, I am at present on a diet that is rather pleasant. The reason for it is an unusual constipation from which I have been suffering for the last six months. Tomorrow, I believe, I will take a dose of pills. I do not feel any particular discomfort, but I certainly shall, if my condition continues. Sister Violante has greatly improved but is still under observation. Sister Giulia[41] gives us a lot to do because she cannot manage at all by herself, and every time she has to get out of bed, three or four of us must be there ready to carry her. I do not believe she will be able to come through: the fever is not breaking and the diarrhea is persistent. I am assisting her incessantly, for it seems to me that now is the time to show my affection to Sister Luisa by relieving her of as many tasks as I possible can.

Vincenzo kept the clock for many days, and since then it works worse than ever. In my opinion the trouble is with the cord, which is too old to run smoothly. Even so, since I cannot do anything myself, I am sending it to you. See what the problem is and, please, mend it. The fault is possibly mine; perhaps I did not know how to handle it. So I have left the weights where they were because I do not know how they should be connected. I pray you, send it back as soon as you can, for these nuns won't leave me alone otherwise.

Sister Brigida would like to remind you about that favor you promised to her, that is, that poor girl's dowry, and I myself would appreciate knowing if Porzia told you anything about what I asked her to do. I will not say what it is for I am afraid to annoy you, so I am only sending a reminder.

I would also like to know if the letter I wrote for Sister Maria Grazia turned out to be to your liking. If not, I could remedy the matter by writing another one. I jotted down that letter in a hurry, because I never have sufficient time for all I have to do. Unfortunately, I cannot take any time away from my sleep, for surely my health would greatly suffer.

I thank you for the loan of the mule to Sister Chiara. I begged for this favor because I did not want her to think that I objected to her being served by you. I am sending back the empty flask. Sister Violante greatly enjoyed the good wine that was in it and she sends her thanks.

When the other day she saw your package of caviar, Sister Arcangela mistook it for the Dutch cheese you usually send for her; so if Your Lordship does not mind, please send some more before the carnival season is over.

Now I feel like chatting and would like to go on and on, but I am afraid of boring you or even worse, tiring you out. So I close, commending myself to you a thousand times, with Sister Luisa and all of us here. May the Lord bless you always.

Your devoted daughter Sister Maria Celeste
January 21, 1630.

XLIII

[Sent to Bellosguardo]

Most beloved Lord and Father:

Our Nora[42] reported to me that you are aware of all my troubles, and, as I do not want always to be the bearer of bad news, I did not go into what has been happening here. But now I can tell you that Sister Luisa, thank God, is well, and Sister Arcangela and I are very well indeed; Sister Chiara is reasonably well, and the two old sisters as usual. May it please God to keep you in a condition as good as I wish; but I do not hope for it, with the weather being so inclement these days. However, as I would like to know how you are any way, I am sending someone with the excuse of bringing you these few pastries to eat at supper during these days of Lent.

Last night Vincenzo had a nice jar of caviar delivered to us, and Sister Arcangela gives her thanks, because caviar is just what she likes, while it does not agree with me. In place of it, I would like to have something with which to make a soup, and also several dried figs, which is what my stomach tolerates. In the past few years you have been spoiling me and made me think that I can openly say what I wish. So I feel confident that you do not mind my asking.

The clock that I sent up and down so many times is now working to perfection. It was all my fault if it did not work. In my attempts to repair it, I must have tightened the cord too much. I sent it to you in a basket covered with a towel, and I have received neither one nor the other. If you by chance find them around the house, please sent them back. I will not write anything more at present, except for sending you greetings on the part of all the people mentioned above. And I pray the Holy God to keep you happy for a long time.

Most devoted daughter Sister Maria Celeste
From San Matteo. February 19, 1630.

XLIV

[Sent to Bellosguardo]

Most beloved Lord and Father:

If I am bold to ask you for favors, I do not want to be too slow in thanking when I receive them. So I say thanks for all the lovely things that last Monday we got from sister-in-law; and that is a package of sweetmeats[43] and the thirteen *cantucci*,[44] which indeed are all very delicious. We are relishing them a little bit at the time. We fully appreciate your kindness and your promptness in always indulging us in all our whims. I have also received some scraps of fabric, which I imagine are coming from Porzia.

And since you like to make certain that I am never left idle, I will tell you that besides my usual activities, I am kept very busy by Mother Superior. Whenever she has some important letter to write, to the governor, for instance, or to the men who work for us here, or such like people, she gives the task to me. This is no simple matter, because the ordinary duties I must perform do not allow me the calm that I would need for these special assignments. So, to make my work easier and in order to get better results, I would very much like you to provide me with a primer of correspondence, as you once said you were going to do. I know you would have done so, had it not slipped your mind.

Yesterday morning Vincenzo was here (perhaps for no more than one hour), together with sister-in-law—and her mother—and from her I heard that you intend to go to Rome.[45] This upset me quite a lot at first, but then I felt assured because I thought that you would not start on a journey if you did not feel up to it. I believe we will see each other before this comes to pass, so I will not say anything more now. I send you my affectionate greetings, with those of all the others here, and pray God to grant you his holy grace.

Your devoted daughter Sister Maria Celeste
From San Matteo. March 14, 1630.

If you have collars that need bleaching, send them, and enjoy these fresh eggs for the love of us.

XLV

[Sent to Bellosguardo]

Most beloved Lord and Father:

I was waiting for the chance to give my Easter greetings to you, as I must, in person. For this reason I put it off until now. But since this was not to be, I am sending my good wishes with this letter, and I want you to know how happy I was to learn that the holiday went by very pleasantly for you, for I assume you to be well, not only physically but also spiritually. I thank God for it. Hearing, however, that you are so deeply immersed in your studies worries me somewhat, because I fear it may be damaging to your health. I would not want you to shorten your life in order to immortalize your fame: a life so revered and held so dear by all of your children, by me in particular. In fact, as I surpass the others in age, so I precede, I am bold to say, and surpass them all in my love for you. I therefore beg you not to tire yourself out and cause harm to yourself as well as affliction and torment to us. I will not say more lest I become tedious, but I send you my heartfelt salutations, together with Sister Arcangela's and with those of all our friends; and I pray the Lord to keep you in his grace.

Most devoted daughter Sister Maria Celeste
San Matteo. April 6, 1630.

XLVI

[Sent to Bellosguardo]

Most beloved Lord and Father:

I am certain Your Lordship is ready and willing to send me what I asked for the other day. If by chance you forgot, I thought it better to remind you of what is needed for tomorrow's lunch with the nuns: a flask of wine, two shapes of ricotta, and something to go after the roast. Not lemons or rosemary bread, as you suggest, but something more substantial and to my liking. We will be waiting for you, sister-in-law and Vincenzo, as you promised. In the meanwhile, praying God to grant you everything you wish, we greet you from the bottom of our hearts.

Your devoted daughter Sister Maria Celeste
April 14, 1630.

XLVII

[Sent to Rome]⁴⁶

Most beloved Lord and Father:

I was very happy to hear, together with Sister Arcangela, that you are well. I am concerned about this more than about anything else in the world. As for myself, I am feeling reasonably well, but not entirely. At the moment I am still on a diet on account of my intestinal blockage. For this reason, and for the many things that at this time we have to take care of in the dispensary, I did not write to you or to the lady ambassador.⁴⁷ Forgive my negligence and see whether the enclosed copy is correct. If not, I will wait for your corrections. Sister Arcangela and all the others are well, except for Sister Violante who has still diarrhea.

The abbess sends her greetings and would like to remind you of what she told you in person, that is, if you get the chance, do try to obtain a donation for the convent; you may want to do so for our good and for love of God, she says. To which I would like to add that it seems a strange thing to me to ask favors of faraway strangers, because if they wanted to help anyone, they would prefer to benefit their own fellow-citizens who are close by. Nonetheless, I am certain that you know how to achieve your intent when the right moment comes. So I warmly entreat you to take care of this business, because we really find ourselves in dire need, and if it were not for some charity we receive now and then we would risk starvation. May the Lord be thanked because notwithstanding our great want, he does not let us suffer, except out of grief, and that is for seeing our dear mother the abbess worry all the time. I especially pity her and wish I could help her and show her my love in some specific way. I would also like to remind you of the reliquiae I asked for. I do not want to be vexing, so I will close, and send you my affectionate greetings with those of all the nuns here. May our Lord keep you safe.

Most devoted daughter Sister Maria Celeste
From San Matteo. May 25, 1630.

XLVIII

[Sent to Bellosguardo][48]

Most beloved Lord and Father:

Just when I was about to write to Your Lordship a letter of lamentation for your delay in coming to visit me, I received your very loving letter, which put an end to my doubts and in fact left me speechless. I can only reproach myself for being too insecure and suspicious. I was afraid that the love you bear for those near to you might have cooled or diminished your affection for us who are absent. But in fact, I recognize my worthlessness and cowardice in this matter, for I should rather harbor generous thoughts and be persuaded that you love us, your daughters, more than anyone else, just as I yield to no one in loving you. I believe that my fear derives from a scarcity of merits in me. But enough with all this now.

We are sorry to hear about your indisposition, but honestly, after making that journey in this kind of weather, it could not have been otherwise. In fact I was surprised to hear that you went to Florence every day. I beg you, then, stay at home and rest for a few days. And do not hurry to come to see us, for we care more about your health than about your visiting us.

Meanwhile, see if by chance you have a rosary left to bring me. I would like to send it to Signora Ortensia, to whom I have not written for quite a while. I did not want to write to her

before writing to you first, but I was overcome by such a lassitude that I was left without even the strength to push a pen, as
they say. But since the weather has started to cool off a bit, I
have been feeling better, thank God. And all the time I pray him
for your good health and well-being, for I care no less for yours
than I do for mine.

Thank you for the wine and the fruit; they were much appreciated. We were keeping these small marzipan cakes (twelve in all)
for the time of your visit, but we have decided to send them to you
before they go stale. The tiny *biscotti* are for little Virginia.[49] In
closing, I give you my affectionate regards together with those of
mother the abbess and the rest of us.

Your devoted daughter Sister Maria Celeste
From San Matteo. July 21, 1630

XLIX

[Sent to Bellosguardo]

Most beloved Lord and Father:

For my good luck, I happen to be able to remedy in part the least of the many misfortunes you said have befallen you; by that I mean your having had two barrels of vinegar go bad. In place of it I can provide you with these two flasks, which I was lucky to get as a special favor. This seems fair to me and so I hope you will accept my good gesture, for I wish I were really able to provide for you in all your needs. Sister Violante, and we too, thank you a lot for the frogs and the cantaloupe. We are greatly enjoying not only the gift in itself but even more the thought of your solicitude in providing it for us.

Yesterday morning Mother Superior ordered me to ask you whether you thought we should send a thank-you note to the very serene grand duke[50] for the gift of money he made to us. Since it was brought here by a worker who lives at Barbadoro, I did not give him a receipt. I did not think of it, and now I pray you to advise me as soon as possible what I ought to do, and at the same time I hope to hear some good news about the request we made yesterday morning. I send you greetings in everybody's name, and pray our Lord to keep you well.

Your devoted daughter Sister Maria Celeste
September 4, 1630.

In one of the vinegar flasks, I have kept a few small roses.

L

[Sent to Florence]

Most beloved Lord and Father:

I did not send a reply back when your last letter arrived because I did not want to detain your servant too long. Now I can thank you for your many kindnesses at leisure. It was really gratifying to give your beautiful plums to Sister Violante. She was so delighted and appreciative! So was Sister Luisa, when I presented her with your peaches, which in fact are the fruit she likes best.

I am mortified to learn that the business solicited in name of Mother Superior did not turn out favorably. Perhaps it was too much to hope for, even with your help. We must be patient and see what result the request made in Rome will have.

Last night a fine deer was delivered to us by order of the very serene grand duchess. You should have seen the excitement and the uproar of the nuns when the present was brought in! I do not think the hunters who caught it could have made that much noise.

Now that the weather will be cooling a little, Sister Arcangela and I, together with our most dear friends, are planning to work in my cell, which is so spacious. Unfortunately, the window is too high and needs repairing, if we are to have a little more light. I would like to send the panes to you to be covered with waxed cloth. This way they won't be a problem when they get old. Would you please let me know if you are willing to do this job for me? I am certain of your kindness, but I fear this is a service becoming woodsmen more than philosophers. So tell me sincerely how you feel about it. In the meanwhile I send you heartfelt greetings, together with those of the abbess and all our friends, and pray Holy God to keep you in his grace.

Your devoted daughter Sister Maria Celeste
September 10, 1630

LI

[Sent to Bellosguardo]

Most beloved Lord and Father:

I am alarmed and deeply worried at the thought of how upset you must be by the sudden death of your poor assistant.[51] I presume you will, and I beg you to with all my heart, use all possible diligence to protect yourself from the current danger. At the same time, I believe you know about all the prophylactics and the remedies considered effective in the present state of emergency, so I will not harp on the subject. Nonetheless, with all due respect and filial confidence, I pray you to see to it that you provide yourself with the most excellent remedy of all, and that is the grace of Almighty God, which can be obtained by means of a sincere contrition and penitence. No doubt this is a most efficacious medicine both for the soul and the body. Indeed, if it is true that in order for us to confront this contagious disease effectively it is essential to get on with our existence in a happy mood, what greater happiness could there be in this life than the one brought about by a good and serene conscience? If we possess this treasure, we certainly will not have anything to fear from danger or from death. God punishes us with these scourges with good cause. We then must try, with his help, to be always ready to accept the blows from his mighty hand, because, after courteously bestowing on us the gift of life, he retains the power to take it away when and how he pleases.

Please accept these few words of mine, for they are offered with sincere affection for you. At the same time I would like you to be aware of my present frame of mind, as I am now willing and ready to pass on to the next world, God be thanked. With every day that goes by, I see more clearly the vanity and misery of our existence, and I also consider that in the other life I would no longer be able to offend God, while I could pray for you more effectively. Perhaps this wish is only a proof of my selfishness. May the Lord, who sees everything, mercifully remedy my deficiency, which is born out of ignorance, and may he grant you all possible consolation.

All of us here are in good health, except Sister Violante who is wasting away slowly. On the other hand, we are troubled by a great penury but, with God's help, not to the point of suffering physically from it.

I would like to know if you have received an answer from Rome in regard to our request for a donation. Signor Corso sent the fifteen pounds of silk, and Sister Arcangela and I have received our share.

It is now the seventh hour of the night, so Your Lordship will excuse any mistake I may have made writing this letter, for during the day I have no time whatsoever. In addition to my usual tasks, I am now teaching plainchant to four young ladies, and, furthermore, on the abbess's order, I supervise the choir for the daily office. This is a rather difficult charge for me, for I have no knowledge of Latin. It is true that I would find these new assignments a great deal more enjoyable if I did not have the obligation to carry on with my usual duties as well. Nonetheless, I derive no small advantage from all this work, because I am never left idle for a single quarter of an hour. Still, I need to sleep a lot on account of my poor troubled head. I really would like to know what your secret is in this matter, for you manage to get away with very little sleep, while I am forced to waste as many as seven hours trying to get some rest.

Lest I become tedious, I will say no more but send you affectionate greetings, on the part of all my usual friends as well.

Your devoted daughter Sister Maria Celeste
October 18, 1630

The little basket in which you received a few pastries a short while ago is not mine, so I would like to have it back.

LII

[Sent to Bellosguardo]

Most beloved Lord and Father:

I had no doubts whatsoever that you would comply with my desire and write for me the letter to be sent to the archbishop, and although you maintain not to have written a good one, it is certainly much better than anything I could have written myself. I am so much obliged for it. And with my thanks I am sending these six quince pears that I have procured recently, for I know you have a special liking for them and have not been able to find any. In fact, there is great scarcity for such fruit at present, as far as I am told. Even so, if the promise made to me is kept, I think I will be able to send you a few more soon.

I would like to know if Vincenzo has gone to Prato after all. I had in mind to write to him about it and ask him not to go, or at least not to leave the house unattended. This behavior of his seems to me very strange, considering what might happen in the current situation.[52] But fearing that no good would come out of telling him, and that I would cause a great fuss instead, I refrained from saying anything. Even a better reason is that I firmly hope that God Almighty will intervene with his Providence wherever men are failing, not for lack of affection, but rather for want of intelligence and consideration. I greet you with love, and so do my friends here. I will accompany you with my poor prayers.

Your most devoted daughter Sister Maria Celeste
October 28, 1630.

LIII

[Sent to Bellosguardo]

Most beloved Lord and Father:

I believe you know better than me that tribulations come to us as a test and proof of our love for God. The more patiently we accept them from his hand, the more certain we can be of holding in reserve a promise of eternal felicity.

I beg you not to do injury to yourself by handling the knife of your present travails and adversities by the blade and against the cut. Take it by the safe side, use it to slice away all the imperfections that you may recognize in yourself, and this way be rid of all possible inner impediments. And then, just as you have penetrated the heavens with a Lyncean's eyesight,[53] you will enter these lower spheres and be able to discover the vanity and fallacy of all our earthly concerns. You will see and experience directly that neither love for children nor earthly pleasures, honors or riches can give us the true contentment, because they are too unstable in themselves; you will also come to realize that we may find true peace only in God, who is our sole final destination. Oh, what will our joy be like when this fragile veil that blinds us is torn away and we shall rise to see that great God face to face? Let us then endeavor, in these few days of life that are left to us, to become worthy of such great and eternal prize! It seems to me, my dear Father and Lord, that you have started on the right path, as long as you continue to avail yourself of all the occasions that you may be offered, especially in doing good to people who recompense you with ingratitude.[54] This kind of action is so much more virtuous and perfect, the more difficult it is to perform. And it seems to me that it brings us closer to God than any other sort of behavior, for we then can experience ourselves what happens to God, because, even though we keep offending his Divine Majesty, he goes on granting us numberless benefits daily. And, if at times, he chastises us, he does so to our greater advantage, just as a good father turns to the rod when he wants to redress his son. That is what is happening at the present time in our poor city of Florence, so that we may make amend through our fear of impending danger.

I do not know if you heard about Matteo Ninci's death, the brother of our Sister Maria Teodora. His brother, Sir Alessandro,[55] wrote to me that Matteo was ill for no more than three or four days, and that he died very much in the grace of God, as far as we can surmise. I believe that all the others in the family are well, though immensely grieved by their great loss. I believe Your Lordship will be distressed by hearing about it, just as we are, because Matteo was a young man very considerate and well behaved indeed.

But, as I do not want to give you only bad news, I will say that the letter I wrote on behalf of Mother Superior to monsignor the archbishop was very welcome, and that we received a courteous answer promising favors and all possible help. Similarly, the two petitions I wrote last week to the very serene duchess and to the dowager duchess have had a good outcome. On All Saints' Day we received a donation of three hundred loaves of bread from the dowager duchess, and we were told that we can send for as many as eight bushels of wheat. This gift has greatly relieved the worry of Mother Superior, who was afraid that we wouldn't have any seed to do our sowing with.

Please forgive me if my prattle gets to be wearisome, but I am encouraged to go on by some signs indicating to me that you take pleasure in my letters. Besides, I have chosen you as my special patron saint (to use one of our expressions), to whom I can confide all my thoughts and with whom I share all my pleasures and displeasures: someone I can always find ready to help me, to whom I can ask not for everything I need—for that would be too much—but for what is most necessary to me at any point in time. Now, for instance, that the cold weather is approaching, I will have to freeze if my patron saint does not run to my rescue by sending me a quilt. The blanket I use at the moment is not mine, and the owner wants it for herself, naturally. The quilt and the blanket you once gave us I was forced to leave to Sister Arcangela, because she wants to sleep alone, and that is fine with me. But all I have left is a serge coverlet, and if I am to wait until I can afford to buy a quilt, I am afraid I will not get one even by next winter. So I turn for help to my patron saint, who is so devoted to me and certainly will not let me down. May it please God (if it is for the best) to keep him safe for me for a long time to come, because besides him I have no one else in the world. One thing I regret, and that is having no way of reciprocating what you do for me! All I can do is incessantly to entreat the Holy God and the Blessed Virgin to reserve a place for you in paradise. This is the best I can come up with in exchange of all the favors you have granted and keep granting to me all along.

Here are two small jars of electuary[56] reputed to be good prophylactics against the plague. The jar with no label on it contains a mixture made with dried figs and walnuts, and compounded with rue, salt, and a good quantity of honey.[57] It is thought to be an excellent preventive if a quantity the size of a walnut is taken in the morning on an empty stomach, with a little Greco or some other good wine to follow. The truth is that we rather overcooked it, and that was because we did not pay enough attention to the figs, which should be just well set. You can take the same quantity of the other mixture, although you may find it slightly unpalatable. Whatever of the two you decide to make use of, we will try to prepare it to perfection next time.

In one of your letters you wrote that you would be sending your telescope to me.[58] I think you forgot all about it, so I am reminding you of it. Also please return the basket in which I sent the quinces so that I can send you more if I can find them. With this I close and commend myself to you with all my heart, together with everyone of us here, as usual.

Your most devoted daughter Sister Maria Celeste
From San Matteo. All Souls' Day, 1630.

LIV

[Sent to Bellosguardo]

Most beloved Lord and Father:

I wish to know if you are well, so I am dispatching someone with the excuse to bring you a small quantity of the water blessed by our mother, Sister Orsola of Pistoia. I have obtained it as a special favor, since the nuns are not allowed to give it to the people outside the convent, and, besides, anyone who has any of it saves it almost as a relic. I pray you accept it in all faith and devotion as a very powerful protection sent by our Lord, who often uses very humble people to show his power and might to greater advantage. That is made clear by this holy mother who, from a poor servant nun as she was who could not even read, managed to rise and govern her convent for many years and restore it to the discipline and order in which we find it today.

Here are four or five letters of hers and other writings of great inspiration. I also have reports written by trustworthy people which give clear indication of her goodness and perfection. I therefore pray you to have confidence in this remedy, because if you show to place so much faith in my miserable prayers, you ought to have much more faith in that blessed soul, and be certain that by her merits you will escape all dangers. So I commend myself to you affectionately, and I will anxiously wait to have news of you.

Your most devoted daughter Sister Maria Celeste
November 8, 1630.

LV

[Sent to Bellosguardo]

Most beloved Lord and Father:

Sunday morning at the fourteenth hour, our Sister Violante passed on to a better life. We may devoutly believe that she has gone to her place of salvation, having suffered such long and trying infirmity with much patience and in conformity with the will of his Holy Majesty. Indeed, for the past month she was reduced to such a debilitated condition that she could not even turn in bed by herself, and only with extreme effort could take a small quantity of food. Death seems to have come to her almost as the desirable final cessation of all suffering. I wanted to tell you about her death earlier, but I could not find the time to write. Even now that I am writing I am in a hurry, so I will add nothing else, except to say that we are all well, thank God, and that I would like to know if you and those few who are left with you are well too, especially little Galileo. I must also thank you for the quilted cover you sent me, which is even too sumptuous for me. I pray the Lord to reward you for all the good things you have done and keep doing for me: may he grant you an increase of grace in this life and of heavenly glory in the next. I commend myself to you with all my heart, together with Sister Arcangela and Sister Luisa.

Your devoted daughter Sister Maria Celeste
From San Matteo. November 26, 1630.

LVI

[Sent to Bellosguardo]

Most beloved Lord and Father:

Seeing Signora Piera was a great relief, because she assured me that you are well.[59] Furthermore, I find that she is a woman of good judgment and discretion, and this puts my mind to rest. Knowing that in times as dangerous as these, you are alone, deprived of all beloved company and assistance, has caused me to worry day and night; so I often lament the distance that prevents my having news of you as frequently as I would like. Nonetheless, I hope that God in his mercy will protect you from all sinister accidents, and to this end I pray him with all my heart. And who is to say that the company of more people would not have placed you at greater risk than you are now? One thing I know: whatever happens to us is due to God's Providence and comes to pass for our greater benefit. This consideration gives me comfort.

This evening we have been ordered by the archbishop to make a list of all our close relatives and hand it to him by tomorrow. Apparently he wants to see to it that all our families contribute to the upkeep of the convent, at least long enough for us to make it through this very harsh winter. I have asked mother the abbess for permission to warn you in advance; as for the rest, I can only recommend this matter to God, and myself to Your Lordship's judgment. I would not want you to be unduly burdened by this emergency measure but I cannot in good conscience prevent their attempt to come to the rescue of this poor beleaguered house. These is one thing, however, you could suggest to the archbishop. What I am going to say is of common knowledge.

It would be useful and appropriate to make many parents pay up the two hundred scudi they still owe for their daughters's dowries.[60] I do not mean only the capital, but also the interest that has accrued in so many years. Among these parents, you understand, is Sir Benedetto Landucci who owes to Sister Chiara, his daughter. If nothing is done about it, I am afraid that you, being his guarantor, or even Vincenzo, will have to pay in his place. If these relatives were asked to close their accounts, the convent would be much better off, more, in fact, than if the families were invited to contribute, because only a few of them could really afford it. The intention of our superiors is very good, and they help us as much as they can, but our need far exceeds their ability to help. On my part, I envy no one in the world except the Capuchin fathers, who are protected from such dealings and anxieties, while we poor nuns must not only work to supply what is needed to the convent, by producing grain and money every year, but are also expected to pay for our personal necessities out of what we manage to earn, which is hardly anything at all. My considered opinion is that the loss is greater than the gain because, by toiling until later at night, we place our health at risk and, besides, consume a great deal of oil, which is so expensive.

Piera told me that you would like to know if we need anything. In that case I would not be shy to ask for some money with which to repay a few small debts that pray on my mind. As for the rest, we are glad to have enough to live by. And so we get on, with God's help.

I see that you do not mention coming to see us anytime soon, and I do not want to annoy you, especially because there would be no pleasure in it, since at present we would not be able to talk as freely as we wanted.[61] I am so pleased that you like the candied fruits. The pieces shaped like quinces were made with a citron I managed to get with great perseverance, of which, after Sister Luisa's suggestion, I processed the hardest part as well, and I call it super citron. The others were prepared in my usual way, which is the way you know. And as I cannot guess which ones you like best, I will keep to the old method unless you tell me otherwise, and I am at your disposal for any specialty you might want to try. I will not go into the list of boxes, phials, and such like things that I would like you to collect for our dispensary, for I already told your governess about it; but I would appreciate you to add the two white plates of mine which you still have. And now I say good night, as it is the ninth hour of the night of December 4, 1630.[62]

Your most devoted daughter Sister Maria Celeste

After you have been to see the archbishop, I would like to know what was said.

LVII

[Sent to Bellosguardo]

Most beloved Lord and Father:

I see that this north wind does not allow you to come here as soon as you had promised; in fact I am afraid it might be bad for your condition. So I am sending someone to see you and deliver these candied citrons, that is the bits made with the rind of the large citron, without the bitter skin. The other bits are made with the rind of the smaller fruit, skin and all. Best of all I think is the big round piece, for which I used much more sugar.

I am planning to get a Christmas present ready for Virginia and for mother Piera. I would like you to send me what I need before the holidays so that my gifts could be ready when the time comes. I would also love to plan a surprise for Sister Luisa, and it would be nice if you contributed. See if around the house you happen to have some leather or colored cloth in sufficient quantity to make a curtain for the door of her cell. The length should be about three yards, and the width slightly less than two. On the curtain I will hang a few trifles to make her laugh, such as a bobbing, a file of matches to light up the lamp during the night, a wax taper, needles and such small things. More than anything else this is to give her a sign of gratitude for the many obligations that I have contracted toward her. If you have something in the house that will do for this purpose, I would be glad to have it; but if you do not find anything, do not go out of the house to look for it, and do not put yourself to any risk whatsoever, for what I most want is for you to be safe, so I beg you to take as much care of yourself as you possibly can.

I have not yet heard anything else about monsignor the archbishop; I would love to know if you have been called. With this, I commend myself to you with all my heart, together with Sister Arcangela and my usual friends. May our Lord keep you safe.

Your devoted daughter Sister Maria Celeste
From San Matteo. December 15, 1630.

LVIII

[Sent to Bellosguardo]

Most beloved Lord and Father:

I had hoped to see you before the beginning of Lent, but as I could not, I would like at least to know how you are in body and spirit. As to the other necessities of life, I am convinced you are well provided for, having already made at your leisure ample provisions, or at least enough for you to go out only with great circumspection, as you did in the past. I would like to be reassured about this, although, for that matter, I do not believe you are willing to go out and far from your nest, especially at this time of the year. May it please the Lord these precautions be sufficient to save all of us from the plague, but especially you, as I hope will be, with God's help. For our Lord does not fail those who firmly confide in him, as it has happened just now to us in the convent. This time, in fact, God has provided us with some very good charity, that is, two hundred four scudi, five lire and four crazie, given, I believe, by the officers of public health, by order of the very serene duchesses, who are showing a great benevolence toward our monastery. Consequently, this month at least, we shall be without much worry, especially our poor mother the abbess, who I believe has obtained this bonus through her prayers and with her begging and recommending herself and the convent to several people.

I prepared this candied ring with the citron you sent a while ago, while the other almond-shaped comfit is made with orange rind. See if you like them. The quince pear was better a few days ago, but I could not find a way to send it. I will write nothing else because I am out of paper; so I send you warm greetings, on the part of my usual friends as well.

Your devoted daughter Sister Maria Celeste
January 14, 1631.

LIX

[Sent to Bellosguardo]

To the most illustrious and most beloved Lord and Father:

Your sorrow in hearing of my poor state of health must be dispelled, for now I can say that I am reasonably well in regard to the indisposition that overtook me a few days ago, and, as far as my old intestinal blockage goes, I believe I will be in need of a more efficacious cure when the suitable time comes. In the meanwhile I shall take good care of myself, as you entreat me to do. Really, I wish you followed yourself the advice you give to me, instead of plunging in your studies with such intensity as to bring irreparable injury to your health.[63] If, when you endeavor to investigate new things, your poor beleaguered body serves your mind well, just as a well-attuned instrument does, you must for that reason give it the rest it needs; otherwise it will become so totally discomfited as to render your intellect incapable even of tasting the food that was grasped with such eagerness.

I thank Your Lordship not only for the two scudi and the other lovely things you sent me, but even more for the generosity and the readiness in doing so, which shows that the greater becomes my need for help, the more desirous you are to come to my rescue.

It pleases me to hear that little Galileo is enjoying good health. During Lent, when the weather improves, I will be happy to see him. I am also glad to read of your surmise that Vincenzo is well,

110

although I do not like the manner in which you came to learn about it; I do not like your not being told by him. Unfortunately, this is the reward of the ungrateful world in which we live.

I am rather embarrassed to be told that you save my letters. I am afraid the great affection you have for me may make them seem to you more skilled than they really are. But let that be as it may; your liking them pleases me enough. And with this I will say à Dieu, and pray God to be always with you, plus all the usual greetings.

Most devoted daughter Sister Maria Celeste
From San Matteo. February 18, 1631.

LX

[Sent to Bellosguardo]

Most beloved Lord and Father:

You have received, no doubt, the letter I wrote to you many days ago, so I will not repeat anything I said there, except to say that I am well, and so are all my friends here, God be thanked. It is true that with all these retreats and fasts that have been going on—it would be more correct to say "that have gone to my head"—I have not been able to receive as frequent news of you as I would have liked. However, these religious observations must come to an end soon, and so we will be able to see you again. In the meanwhile I wish to know how you are, which is what I most care for, and also whether you have heard from Vincenzo and from sister-in-law.

I am sending back two empty flasks together with these few spice cakes, which I think you will like, provided too much cooking has not made them, as I fear, too hard for your teeth. The rainy weather did not permit me to make the rosemary jam I had planned, but as soon as I can get some flowers nice and dry, I shall, and will send it to you.

I commend myself most warmly to you, together with Sister Arcangela and the rest of us, as usual. I pray our Lord to keep you in his holy grace. Please give one little kiss to young Galileo for me.

Most devoted daughter Sister Maria Celeste
From San Matteo. March 9, 1631.

LXI

[Sent to Bellosguardo]

Most beloved Lord and Father:

Your Lordship's letter caused me great anguish for several reasons, first because it told me about the death of Uncle Michelangelo.[64] I am indeed grieved by it, not only for the loss of him, but also because of the added financial burden that will derive to you, and this will not be, I fear, the least of your problems or, rather, tribulations.

However, you must consider that since God has been generous with you as far as longevity and mental prowess are concerned, far more than with your brother and sisters, it is fitting that you use them according to the will of the Divine Majesty whose gift they are. So, if you can find a position for Vincenzo that would make it possible for him to earn some money, the bother and the expense to you will be lessened, and his excuses for complaining will have diminished.

For this reason then, my dear Lord and Father, since you were brought and kept in this world for the benefit of many, see that your own son is the first of those who are benefitted by you. What I mean is that you ought to find a starting situation from which he could advance on his own; as for the rest, I know there is no need of recommendation. I mention this matter only in your interest, because I wish you to live in harmony with Vincenzo and his wife,

114

and so be allowed to enjoy your own life in peace—which I do not doubt will happen, if you will do him this good service, just as he so ardently wishes. At least this is what I have been able to gather every time I spoke to him.

I deeply regret not being able to please you in the matter of having Virginia here, as much as I would like to for the love I owe her, because she is such an amusement and comfort to you. Our superiors have clearly stated that they will in no way allow us to take in girls, neither as nuns nor as novices, because the convent is very poor, as Your Lordship knows well, and we can hardly provide the living necessities for ourselves who are already here, let alone adding more mouths to feed. The scarcity of food must be the reason for their refusal and for the warning they gave to all relatives and friends. Consequently, I dare not to ask for an exception either to Mother Superior or anyone else. You can be sure that I feel a keen regret for not being able to comply with your wishes; on the other hand, I see no way out.

I am also sorry to hear that you are not feeling well. If it were possible, I would be ready to take all your pains upon me, but since that cannot be, I will not fail to favor you in my devotions, in which I always place you before myself. So may it please God to answer our prayers. My health has been so satisfactory lately that I have started observing Lent, and I hope I will be able to complete my observance to the end. So do not worry about sending me things, which, really, seem more fitting the carnival season than a time of fasting. I thank you for the things you have already given me, and in closing I commend myself to you, together with Sister Arcangela and all our friends.

Most devoted daughter Sister Maria Celeste
From San Matteo. March 11, 1631.

If you do not know what to do with the leftover meat, I certainly know to whom to distribute it. The one you sent was very welcome. So when the chance arises, do send it.

LXII

[Sent to Bellosguardo]

Most beloved Lord and Father:

A thousand thanks for the lovely things you had delivered here. They were very welcome, for this year is a very penurious one and we are spending Lent very meagerly, although when one is in good health one can easily tolerate everything else.

We greatly long for yours and little Galileo's visit, and hope it will be at the earliest. Meanwhile, I take pleasure in knowing that you are very well, while I wish to express my regret again for not being able to do anything about Virginia and comply with Your Lordship's wishes in that respect. Hopefully the good Lord will provide in some other way. That Vincenzo should be afraid to catch the plague from you will turn out to be very convenient, for one does not take money from people suspected of carrying the infection; so his fear will prevent him from asking for any. I warmly commend myself to you and pray God to keep you healthy.

Your most devoted daughter Sister Maria Celeste
From San Matteo. March 12, 1631.

LXIII

[Sent to Bellosguardo]

Most beloved Lord and Father:

I am not surprised by the very warm affection you have for me, for many are the signs and countersigns that you give. What I am amazed at is that your love is so powerful that allows you to guess what my favorite dish is, and also which one, among all Lent preparations, is more fitting to my condition. I am endlessly grateful for it and look forward to enjoying it with redoubled pleasure, for it was prepared by those hands that I love and worship. And since you want me to say what else I would like, I am bold to ask for something to eat at supper, and, for the rest, I pray you, do not worry about it, because if I need anything, I will make myself clear, knowing that I can do so freely.

I am looking forward to seeing you and the child, provided it is a weekday, for there would be no point in traveling so far on a holy day and get here for nothing.

You can imagine how pleased I would be if the favor you plan to ask from monsignor the archbishop could be obtained; but at this moment I cannot decide what it should be. I will talk to the abbess and will let you know what I have been able to make out of it. In closing I commend myself to you many times over, and I pray our Lord to keep you in good health.

Your devoted daughter Sister Maria Celeste
From San Matteo. March 13, 1631.

LXIV

[Sent to Bellosguardo]

Most beloved Lord and Father:

The report I received from the abbess, regarding the petition you wrote to me about the other day, is that it would unquestionable be the nuns' unanimous desire to obtain that favor from monsignor the archbishop not only for the fathers but for the brothers as well. However, she believes it more advisable to wait until Easter has gone by before presenting our petition. By then, you will have been here and will have had the chance to talk with the abbess herself, who is indeed a prudent and discreet person although very shy.

I am sending back the collars that you wanted to have whitened. They are so worn out that it was impossible to restore them to perfection. If you need anything else, remember that I derive no greater satisfaction in the world than being busy in your service, just as you seem to find no greater pleasure than in pleasing me and in satisfying all my requests, for you do attend to each of my needs with a great deal of care indeed.

Thank you for all your kindness and in particular for the gifts you sent to us recently by the hand of our bailiff, which were two packages, one of almonds and the other one of sweetmeats and some *biscotti*. We will enjoy them greatly, thanks to your good heart. For my part, I am presenting you with a poor woman's gift:

that is to say, with this jar of jam, which I hope will help assuage your head, although you could do it better yourself if you avoided getting exhausted with so much studying and writing. The little things in the basket are for Virginia. I won't say anything more because time is running out, except that in name of the usual nuns I greet you affectionately and pray our Lord God to grant you his holy grace.

Most devoted daughter Sister Maria Celeste
From San Matteo. March 17, 1631.

LXV

[Sent to Bellosguardo]

Most beloved Lord and Father:

As usual, the work in the dispensary has kept and still keeps me so occupied that I do not have sufficient time to say anything for the present except to apologize for my long delay in sending someone to see you. Now that I can, I dispatch a messenger to learn if you are well and if you have news of Vincenzo and sister-in-law, that is, if you think that they will spend the Holy Easter with you. This, I believe, would please you a lot, and me too, for the love of you. These pastries here are only a few, but they will do, I believe, since you do not have anyone to share them with, except little Galileo. He can play with the pine cones, which are the entire share the gardener nun gave to me and to Sister Arcangela.

I am not sending back the dish in which the spinach arrived because it is not completely empty. The spinach is so good that I have been eating a smidgeon at a time. I send you greetings on the part of all of us and pray our Lord to give you everlasting happiness.

Your devoted daughter Sister Maria Celeste
From San Matteo. April 11, 1631.

LXVI

[Sent to Bellosguardo]

Most beloved Lord and Father:

If your letter had not reassured me that your illness is not serious, I would certainly worry much more than I do at present. In fact, since you tell me to be rapidly improving, I am beginning to hope that I will be able to see you totally recovered in not too long a time, just as you have promised. Vincenzo brought us two dozens eggs and half a lamb, and we thank you. We are even more grateful for the four piastre, for they arrive in time of great necessity. At this moment, Piera is asking for permission to leave, so I propose to write at greater length some other time. For now, I commend myself to you from the bottom of my heart, joined in this by the others. May our Lord be always with you.

Your most devoted daughter Sister Maria Celeste
From San Matteo. April 22, 1631.

LXVII

[Sent to Bellosguardo]

To the most illustrious and most beloved Lord and Father:

The other day, I heard from Piera that Your Lordship was feeling rather listless and with no desire to eat, so I have been trying to think what remedy I could send you to stimulate your appetite. I heard some doctors say that the syrup called Oxilacchara[65] is excellent to this purpose, so I have made a small quantity of it and I am sending it for you to try. It cannot possibly hurt you, for the ingredients are none other than sugar, strong pomegranate wine, and a small quantity of vinegar. It is true that my cooking has perhaps caused the mixture to thicken a trifle too much; even so, you can take two or three spoonfuls in the morning, and, if you want to mitigate its harshness somewhat, you may dilute it with a little cinnamon water. If you have run out of it, I will send you some more, provided you return the little flask in which it arrived. The candied morsels were made with all the citron you sent, and I think they are good. If I could guess what else you might like, I would not omit any effort to provide it, not only to please you but also myself, because busying myself in your service is what I cherish most. I beg you, if you need anything, do not deprive me of this pleasure, and also let me know how your state of health is at present. This said, I pray God to grant you all goodness, and I commend myself to you with affection, together with my friends.

Most devoted daughter Sister Maria Celeste
From San Matteo. April 25, 1631.

LXVIII

[Sent to Bellosguardo]

Most beloved Lord and Father:

As far as I was able to find out, the priest of Monteripaldi has no jurisdiction over Signora Dianora Landi's villa, except in one respect. What I clearly understood is that this property represents the endowment of a chapel in Santa Maria del Fiore, and that is why Signora Dianora finds herself in litigation. From the carrier of this letter, who is a very shrewd woman and knows people all over Florence, you could find out who initiated the lawsuit—she knows the man—and then from him you could learn more about the whole business. Furthermore, I have heard that Mannelli's house has not yet been disposed of, but the intention[66] is indeed to rent it. This is a beautiful place, and I am told it enjoys the best situation in the village. I believe you will not lack the necessary connections to obtain what both you and I ardently desire. Perhaps from the same woman you will be able to get a few addresses.

I had accepted the vinegar for the elixir I am preparing because ours did not seem to be of the quality needed. Since Your Lordship was kind enough to let me have the wine in exchange of it, I thank you. After that, I will wait to hear whether you are satisfied with our preparation, and this will be next time you avail yourself of our services, for Sister Luisa and the other friends in the dispensary made me understand that you will do so soon. In theirs and in Sister Arcagela's name I salute you affectionately, and pray our Lord for your true happiness.

Your devoted daughter Sister Maria Celeste
From San Matteo. May 18, 1631.

LXIX

[Sent to Bellosguardo]

Most beloved Lord and Father:

Now that a good occasion presents itself, it is my utmost desire to give, with your help, some sign of acknowledgment and of gratitude for the many obligations that I have toward Sister Luisa. At present she finds herself in the necessity of procuring a loan of twenty-four scudi until the end of July, so I would like you to do her the favor of lending the money, if it is possible, and I believe it is. If it is true, as I know indeed it is, that Your Lordship wishes to comply with all my desires, you may believe that the present one would give me the greatest possible satisfaction. Sister Luisa is a person who maintains her side of the bargain, and, being able to rely on her income, she will in fact return the money earlier rather than after the prescribed term of two months. In truth, if it were otherwise, I would not ask you, for I should not like to cause Your Lordship any problem, as, to my great regret, happened in the past. I shall not insist then, knowing well that there is no point in extending myself in longer entreaties with a person who has greater desire to benefit me than I have of being benefitted. I shall then wait to be fully satisfied. Meanwhile let me tell you my pleasure when I heard that Monsignor Rinuccini was elected archbishop.[67] This turn of events is both in your interest and in that of the convent, as we shall have the opportunity to consider together.

I wonder if the two potions I made for you were to your satisfaction, for you haven't said anything. And since you did not send the aloe and the rhubarb for the papal pills,[68] I am letting you have two dozens of ours, just as in the past, and I propose to make some especially for you anytime you like. The citrons are magnificent, and with the help of Sister Luisa I shall try to make some very good morsels as well so that he who has given may be willing to give again. In the meanwhile I thank you for these and also for the crystal jars, which were greatly welcome. I pray our Lord to give you all true goodness, and I commend myself to you with my usual friends, particularly Sister Arcangela, who feels rather poorly these days.

Most devoted daughter Sister Maria Celeste
From San Matteo. May 29, 1631.

LXX

[Sent to Bellosguardo]

To the most illustrious and most beloved Lord and Master:

Sister Luisa has begged me to thank you on her behalf as warmly as I can, both for your sympathy and for the help you so readily and courteously have given her. But since I know myself totally incapable of it, I shall not talk about it, trusting that you will be more pleased to hear the following confession. My obligation to you is now greater than ever and my desire is to avoid being ungrateful for the almost endless number of favors I have received from you. Unfortunately, being so poor, I can give no other sign of gratitude than express my feelings. It is true that this last favor of yours surpasses in my opinion all the previous ones, because it proves that your generosity and love are ready to benefit not only me but also the people with whom I have ties of affection and gratitude. And this I consider a double favor. For this reason I wish to replace my dear Sister Luisa in the obligation she may pretend to have toward you.

These candied tidbits here have turned out to be the best looking I have made so far, and I believe they are also the tastiest. I would not want you to give them all away; there are eight and I would like you too to savor them. As you know, Sister Arcangela is on a special diet. The doctor has prescribed the Tettuccio water[69] for her, but in a small quantity because she is very weak.

Now, as this medication requires a nourishing diet, and I am very short of money, I would like you to let me have a pair of chicken to prepare a good soup on Friday and Saturday as well. Sister Chiara too is confined to bed, so what with this and the work in the dispensary, I have put aside altogether any idea of free time. I would in fact be totally crushed by overwork if Sister Luisa did not, God bless her, come to my help and give me a hand with everything that needs to be done. I send you my greetings, on her part and on the part of Sister Arcangela as well, and I pray God to keep you in good health for yours and our benefit.

Most devoted daughter Sister Maria Celeste
From San Matteo. June 4, 1631.

LXXI

[Sent to Bellosguardo]

Most beloved Lord and Father:

Vincenzo was here on Sunday morning, and, if I remember correctly, he said that he had come to see Perini's house which is for sale; and, as far as I understand, and you can find out from Vincenzo himself, the buyer has all the advantage. As I wish nothing but your happiness (I know how much you would like to live near us) as well as Vincenzo's and ours, I write to entreat you not to let this opportunity escape; the house is near us and God knows when another as good as this will be on the market again. One can see that the people who own property around here never want to let go of it, except in extreme necessity, and that is what is happening to Perini and to Mannelli. The latter's place, I understand, has already been rented. If you decide to come and look at the house, you could pay us a visit at the same time. Meanwhile, I can say that I am feeling well, but I cannot say the same for Sister Arcangela, who is reduced to such a poor state as to spend the whole day in bed. Her condition is not alarming, but I believe that if she had not been taken care of from the start, she could have developed some serious illness. The chickens you sent for her have arrived and I thank you no end. I pray our Lord to give you good health and commend myself to you, together with my usual friends.

Most devoted daughter Sister Maria Celeste
From San Matteo. June 10, 1631.

LXXII

[Sent to Bellosguardo]

Most beloved Lord and Father:

By a stroke of luck Sister Luisa has come into her income earlier than expected, and so she is quickly returning the twenty-four scudi she owed you. She insists she will never be able to repay the debt of gratitude to you, which will be everlasting, nor does she want to; and says that she cannot reciprocate your kindness and solicitude except with the coin of a heartfelt regard for you and for us as well. Of this she gives proof every day whenever I am in need of something; she could do no more for me if she were my mother. She has placed these pastries in the basket for you, with prayer to enjoy them for love of her.

Sister Arcangela keeps to her bed with much lassitude and pains, but only a few lines of temperature. It is my impression that it will take much longer for her to recover completely, if she ever will. The last time he was here to see her, the doctor ordered to massage her stomach with some of the duke's rubbing ointment and with some nutmeg oil as well. Since we have scarcity of both, I would like you to provide us with a small quantity of each.

You will find here two empty flasks. Truly, my illness knocked me so, that I would not have managed so well without the white wine, forced, as I was, to live on soups and poultices. But strengthened by such good drink, they did me a lot of good.

I would be pleased to know if the purchase of the house you went to see can be agreed on. I should like it very much and I think it would be a fine and comfortable place for your family to be in. I do not need anything else for the time being, so I send you affectionate greetings with those of my usual friends here and I pray the Holy God to favor you always.

Most devoted daughter Sister Maria Celeste
From San Matteo. July 1631.[70]

LXXIII

[Sent to Bellosguardo]

To the most beloved Lord and Father:

So strong is my desire to have you come to live near us that I always try to find out if there is any place around here for rent. A few days ago I have heard that there is a villa for rent in Pian dei Giullari belonging to Signor Esaù Martellini, whose grounds extend to the convent. I am writing to you about it so you can find out whether the house is to your liking. You cannot imagine how much I would love this to be: with such an arrangement we would not be left without news of you for long stretches of time, as happens now, a situation I can hardly bear. I face and accept this painful inconvenience, and, together with a few other annoyances, I place it in the bundle of other numerous mortifications that I wouldn't care to mention. So I adjust the best I can to God's will. I am convinced, moreover, that you too have no shortage of bothers and worries, certainly greater than my own, and for this reason I keep quiet.

Sister Arcangela, who gave me so much worry, is improving a lot, thank God, and although still weak and weary, she has began to get up for short periods of time. She would like to eat some marinated fish, so I beg you to get some for these coming days of fasting. In the meanwhile, take care of yourself in this hot summer, and please write me a line. I send affectionate greetings from all of us as usual, and I pray our Lord to grant you his grace.

Most devoted daughter Sister Maria Celeste
From San Matteo. August 12, 1631.

LXXIV

[Sent to Bellosguardo]

Most beloved Lord and Father:

We are disappointed that the weather has deprived us of the pleasure of gathering all together here with Your Lordship today. God willing, a new occasion will present itself soon. Meanwhile I am looking forward to the time when I shall have you always near me, and I understand that might be soon, from what Piera told me. I pray you to pursue your intent and get on with your plan, and, with God's help, all obstacles will be overcome.

Tonight I will share with my friends the good provisions you sent me, but I won't give away much of the ricotta. I thank you on everybody's behalf and commend myself to you from the bottom of my heart.

Your devoted daughter Sister Maria Celeste
From San Matteo. August 27, 1631.

LXXV

[Sent to Bellosguardo]

Most beloved Lord and Father:

If the trust one places in people is the measure and sign of one's love for them, then Your Lordship can have no doubt that I love you with all my heart, as in fact is the case: for such is my trust and confidence in you that at times I fear I might exceed the limit of modesty and filial respect, the more so for knowing that you are burdened by many expenses and nuisances. Nonetheless, as certain as I am that you care to meet my necessities just as much as those of anyone else, even your own, I am emboldened to ask you to free me of a worry that has been gnawing at me for some time. That is a debt of five scudi I have incurred into in the past four months, on account of Sister Arcangela's illness, when I was obliged to spend extravagantly, considering our financial situation. And now that I am facing the emergency of repaying that sum, I turn to the person who I know can and wants to help me.

I would also appreciate receiving a flask of your white wine, which I intend to strengthen with a good measure of minerals for Sister Arcangela, although I believe the stock she takes in the remedy will do her more good than the remedy itself.

I am in a great hurry now and I cannot add anything else, except to say that I would like these marzipan cakes to be to your taste, and I commend myself to you.

Your devoted daughter Sister Maria Celeste
From San Matteo. August 30, 1631.[71]

LXXVI

[Sent to Rome][72]

To the most illustrious and most beloved Lord and Father:

The Bocchineri brothers have passed all your letters on to me, and I am quite content with this because I imagine how difficult it must be for you to write. I did not write myself before because I first wanted to have news of your arrival in Rome. When I read in your last letter that you must wait many days in so ugly a place, and deprived of all comforts besides, I was overcome with sorrow.[73] Nonetheless I draw consolation from learning that although without inner and outer solace, you are in a satisfactory physical condition. Thank God for it. It is my firm hope that he will grant us the favor of your return to Florence in spiritual contentment and in bodily fitness. In the meanwhile I urge you to keep in as good cheer as you possibly can, and put your trust in the Lord, who never forsakes those who confide in him.

Sister Arcangela and I are well, but not Sister Luisa, who, since the day you left, has been in bed with those terrible pains of hers. This situation provides me with the chance of getting my mind off the thought of your being away. Worrying about it would have been a big strain on me, if it were not for the necessity of keeping in motion all day long in order to give Sister Luisa her medication and all the help she needs. Signor Rondinelli [74] has not yet come to enjoy the comfort of your house, as you have offered him to do, and said that court litigations have made it impossible so far. Our father confessor, on the other hand, does not omit any chances to avail himself of your invitation. He sends greetings, and the same do the abbess and all my friends here. Sister Arcangela and I incessantly pray our Lord to guard and look over you.

The enclosed letter was found by Giuseppe[75] on Monday, at the place where your mail is usually delivered.

Most devoted daughter Sister Maria Celeste
From San Matteo at Arcetri. February 5, 1633.

LXXVII

[Sent to Rome]

To the most illustrious and most beloved Lord and Father:

Your letter of February 10th was delivered on the 22nd, and by this time I believe you must have received another letter of mine, as well as one from our father confessor, and so by now you know in some detail what you wanted to know. Since no letter has arrived to announce your arrival in Rome (you can imagine with what trepidation I am waiting for it), I write again, not only to tell you how anxious I am about it,[76] but also to send you the enclosed order of payment which was served to you at your house by a young man four or five days ago and was picked up by Francesco Rondinelli. When he gave it to me, Signor Rondinelli advised to pay it immediately, without waiting for the creditor to take further action. He said that in no way should one disobey such injunction, and offered to deal with the matter himself. So this morning I gave him the six scudi, which he does not want to pay to Vincenzo[77] but prefers to deposit at the court until you advise us what to do.

Signor Francesco is indeed a very nice and discreet person, and never stops exaggerating the obligation he has toward you for the chance of making use of your house. From Piera I learned that he deals very kindly with her and Giuseppe even in the matter of food, and I too provide to their needs as you ordered me to do.

The boy[78] tells me that this coming Easter he will be in need of new shoes and new socks. I was planning to make his socks with some strong thread, with flax I think. It was also my idea to buy a small quantity of cotton and have Piera weave a coarse cloth for the kitchen, but she tells me that several times you mentioned buying a bale of linen yourself. So I shall withdraw from the case and wait until you tell me what you want to be done.

Now that the moon is full Giuseppe's father will prune the vines in your orchard. I understand he will be sufficient to the task, and Signor Rondinelli will help him. I have also heard that the lettuce is coming up very nicely and I told Giuseppe to pick it and take it to the market before it is totally wrecked by thieves. From the sale of seventy bitter oranges we got four lire, quite a reasonable price, it seems, for a fruit of such little use. The sweet oranges were two hundred and were sold for fourteen crazie per one hundred.

Out of one of the barrel that you left open, Signor Rondinelli draws some wine to drink at night, and this is also good for the wine, which I understand keeps very well. As to the small quantity left of the old one, I ordered it poured into flasks and told Piera they ought to start drinking it when their little keg is empty, because Sister Arcangela and I have received some fairly good wine from the convent and, as we are enjoying good health, have not made much use of it so far.

I keep giving Brigida a giulio every Saturday for I truly believe this to be an excellent charity. She is a very good girl and in extreme need.

Sister Luisa, thank God, is feeling much better but is still on a special regimen. Realizing how concerned you are about her and how much you love her, she sends you endless thanks. And since you declare that you love her as much as I do, she wishes on her part to stand up to the challenge and surpass both of us in loving, because her feeling, she says, proceeds from the same cause, and that is I. I therefore exalt and glory in such gracious contest, because I thereby see quite clearly how strong is the love of both of you for me, which keeps overflowing to the point that it begins to expand exponentially between the two people who are loved and revered by me above all other mortal beings.

Tomorrow it will be thirteen days since the death of Sister Virginia Canigiani, who was in critical condition the last time I wrote to you. In the meanwhile Sister Maria Grazia del Pace has taken ill with a very malignant fever. She is a really peaceful and good-hearted nun, the oldest of the three nuns who play the organ, and the teacher of the Squarcialupi sisters. We are all upset at the thought of her dying, for the doctor has given her up. This is as much as I have to say for the moment. I will write again as soon as I receive some letters from you (they should be in Pisa by now, where the Bocchineris are at present). In the meanwhile I send you my heartfelt wishes from the same nuns as always, namely from Sister Arcangela, Signor Rondinelli, and from Doctor Ronconi, who asks me news of you every time he comes here. May our Lord God favor and keep you for ever safe.

Most devoted daughter Sister Maria Celeste Galilei

From San Matteo. February 26, 1633.

Signor Rondinelli has just come back from Florence and tells me that he spoke with the secretary of the council who said that we must pay the six scudi directly to Signor Landucci instead of depositing them at the chancery. So we shall, although I gave in only after some resistance, having no instructions from you on this matter.

LXXVIII

[Sent to Rome]

Most beloved Lord and Father:

Yesterday morning Signor Mario Guiducci[79] sent a servant of his to deliver your letters. The letter you addressed to Signor Mario was specially delightful to read and was returned to him immediately. The other I gave to the father confessor who, I believe, will answer to you promptly. I take courage in learning that so far your affair is going smoothly and quietly and I thank the Lord no end for it. The calm with which the whole business is being carried out promises a happy and prosperous outcome, and so I hope it will be, with the divine help and intercession of the Blessed Virgin.[80]

You must have received my letter by now. What happened since I wrote it is as follows. In your name Signor Rondinelli consigned the six scudi to Vincenzo Landucci, who came to get them in person. Sister Luisa has had no pain for several days and shows a satisfactory improvement. For ten days Sister Arcangela has been suffering from a terrible ache in the shoulder and in the left arm, but with the help of some pills and an enema the discomfort has diminished quite a lot. Giuseppe too is in pain, from his stomach and from spleen enlargement, so he cannot continue his observance of Lent, and Signor Rondinelli keeps an eye on him too. And finally, our Maria Grazia, the organist, who I told you was seriously ill, died. She was fifty-eight or sixty years old, and we were all upset about it.

Piera is well, the vines in the orchard have been attended to; and we got half a scudo from the lettuce sold so far. I have nothing else to report, except that I run from pillar to post all day long, without a moment of rest, and that, notwithstanding everything, I enjoy very good health. This well-being I would very willingly share with you, or, better still, I would exchange for your indisposition so that you may go free of all your terrible pains. I am waiting instruction regarding other money to give to Landucci this current month, because I do not want to make a mistake, nor would I like to incur into extra expenses, as it happened last time. By that I mean 6.13, plus 4 lire which were the amounts we had to disburse on account of the order that was served on you.

You can seal my letter to the lady ambassador yourself after reading it. And with this I close and commend myself to you with all my heart, together with the usual people here.

Your most devoted daughter Sister Maria Celeste
From San Matteo. March 5, 1633.

LXXIX

[Sent to Rome]

Most illustrious and beloved Lord and Father:

Your last letter, delivered to me by Signor Andrea Arrighetti,[81] cheered me a lot, both because I hear that you are keeping in a satisfactory state of health and because it reassures me of the good outcome of your affair just as my desire and my love for you had forecast to me.[82] Things being as they are, the time of your return seems to be getting more and more remote. I nonetheless consider it my good fortune to be able in this case to renounce my desire in the hope it will rebound to your benefit and to your greater reputation, for I love you more than I love myself. What reassures me even more is knowing that you are treated with all honor and comfort by those extraordinary people, and in particular by the excellent lady of the house.

Both Sister Arcangela and I would regard a visit from this lady a distinguished honor and a great pleasure. We would welcome it more than you can imagine and more than I could say in so many words. As to staging a comedy for her to see, I could not say. We would have to decide according to the time of her visit, but I dare say, if she wants to see us perform, it would be safe, when you speak to her, to let her infer whatever would be best for her to believe.

Father Benedetto's visit will be welcome just as much, for he is such an illustrious personage and so attached to Your Lordship.[83]

148

Please return his greetings redoubled for us. I would like to have some news of that Anna Maria, for whom you had such glowing praises when you last returned from Rome. I have been interested in her since I first heard from you how skilled and how worthy a person she is.[84]

Sister Arcangela is much better, but her arm less so. Sister Luisa is reasonable well but still on a strict regimen. As for myself, I am fine, I am serene and in continuous motion, except for the seven hours of the night that I can hardly ever give to uninterrupted sleep, on account of my miserable head, which is perennially congested and not leaving me free of pain for one single moment. Nonetheless I never omit my debt of praying for you, and entreat God to grant you spiritual health foremost, and after that all the things you reasonably desire.

I shall say nothing more now, except that I urge you to be patient with me if I have bored you to excess and to take into account that in this letter I have been summarizing all that I would have written in a week.

I send my affectionate greetings, to which I add those of my usual friends. And the same from Signor Rondinelli.

Most affectionate daughter Sister Maria Celeste
From San Matteo at Arcetri. March 12, 1633.

LXXX

[Sent to Rome]

To the most illustrious and most beloved Lord and Father:

Yesterday morning Signor Mario, who is always so considerate, sent to me all the letters he received from you. I have delivered two to the persons they were meant for. Thank you for warning me about the error in my letter to the lady ambassador. From her I have received a most courteous answer. Among other things, she tells me that I should persuade you to make a free use of her house and dispose of it as it were your own, for she is very eager for you to be at perfect ease and as comfortable as possible. I am writing back to her asking for a favor, as you will see. If you think proper for me to advance that request, I shall be pleased; if not, I will submit to your judgment. But indeed, either through the lady ambassador or some other connection of yours, I would very much like to obtain this favor, just as I would like you to bring me a gift when you come back—and I really hope your return will not be far off.

I believe in Rome there are plenty of good paintings, so I would like you to bring me a small picture, the size of the paper enclosed. I would like the kind that can be opened and closed like a book, and with two figures: an Ecce Homo [Christ on the cross] on one side and the Virgin on the other. But I would like them to be full of piety and devotion. I do not want any decoration; a simple frame will do, for all I want is to keep it by me all the time.

I am certain Signor Rondinelli will write to you, so it would be a good idea if, in your reply, you thanked him for the many kind thoughts he has had from time to time toward us during this Lenten season, in particular because he was here to dinner last night and insisted that we should eat with all of them, and spend the day contentedly together. He seemed especially considerate of Sister Arcangela, whose arm is slowly improving.

For several days now, Sister Orietta has been ailing with an infection of the kidneys and has not been able to move about at all, so the office of convent provisioner is now on my shoulders. With this and other tasks, I am reduced to do the writing at midnight and, being very sleepy, I am afraid I have written some blunders. I am greatly pleased to learn that you are well, and pray God to keep you always so. I salute you on the part of all my friends, and also in name of Doctor Ronconi, who inquires about you insistently.

Most devoted daughter Sister Maria Celeste
From San Matteo. March 19, 1633.

LXXXI

[Sent to Rome]

To the most illustrious and beloved Lord and Father:

Last Saturday I was able to read the letter you sent to Signor Andrea Arrighetti. What was especially pleasing to me was learning that not only you continue to enjoy good health but that, with it, your spirits are improving, and a quick and peaceful solution of your affair may be expected soon. For all this, I thank the Lord, for it is to him that we owe these favors.

It was also my pleasure to read that Your Lordship has handed my letter to our most excellent lady ambassador, from which I infer that my making that request was not considered improper, as I had feared. Now that with incomparable courtesy you promise to apply all diligence in securing the favor, I can hope for an advantageous outcome, and I would therefore appreciate our giving the lady ambassador my regards.

I furthermore would like you to perform one more service, not for me but for Sister Arcangela. In three weeks, which is to say on the last day of the month, she will leave the office of provisioner, for which she has spent so far one hundred scudi and more. As each provisioner must leave in the till twenty-five scudi as a deposit for the nun who will be chosen for the same office after her, having no other resources to fall on, I would like, with your permission, to draw the sum needed from the amount you left with me. In this way Sister Arcangela's ship might reach safe harbor, while in truth, without your help, it will not manage to navigate even halfway. There is no need for me to exaggerate a bit, for all becomes clear if I say that all the good things we enjoy—and indeed we have enjoyed many—and all we may hope and desire to receive in the future, we receive and hope to receive only from you, from your extraordinary love and consideration for us. Certainly, it is because of your love that, in addition to finding, in performance of your duty, a place for us to live, you never forgot to satisfy all our needs in a most benign manner, whenever we asked for it, and whatever it might have entailed. No doubt Your Lordship can see that God is rewarding you for your goodness to us. May it also please him to keep you safe and prosperous and all of us happy for a very long time.

The excessive pain I feel in one tooth prevents me from writing any further, so I will not give you other news, except that I shall say that Giuseppe is getting better, and we are all well. We send you affectionate greetings, to which we add those of Piera and all the others.

Most devoted daughter Sister Maria Celeste
From San Matteo. April 9, 1633.

LXXXII

[Sent to Rome]

To the most illustrious and most beloved Lord and Father:

I believe you wanted me to feel mortified during this holy week of sorrow and therefore have stopped writing. I cannot convey you the dismal feeling this situation arouses in me.[85] Although I am in a very great haste, I cannot omit sending you a few lines with seasonal good wishes. May the generous hand of the Lord regale you with an Easter full of spiritual joy, good health, and worldly happiness, as I hope and trust he will.

At present, thanks to God, we are all in good health here, with the exception of our Giuseppe, who will have to go to the hospital soon after the holidays, to take care of his fever and his spleen, which is very swollen. I am trying to see whether, with the help of our abbess, he can be admitted to the Bonifazio hospital, where he will be treated better than in any other. Piera is well and sends her greetings, and I do the same from the bottom of my heart, together with the usual nuns. Please remember that you owe me the answer to three letters.

Most devoted daughter Sister Maria Celeste
From San Matteo at Arcetri. On Holy Saturday, 1633.

LXXXIII

[Sent to Rome]

Most beloved Lord and Father:

From the two letters that I have had from you this week I understand that your affair is progressing satisfactorily. You can imagine how happy I am about it, and I thank God for it. Yesterday there was applause and general rejoicing here for the favor obtained by the very excellent lady ambassador. I wrote these few lines of thanks, but they can hardly express the gratitude I feel toward her for the many favors I have received. I can perform only as well as I can, not how I ought to. I wrote to Signor Giovanni Rinuccini for the purpose you told me to, and, in reply, he says that we should not deal with the matter now and that he will let me know when the appropriate time comes.

Apparently in Florence the epidemic has spread quite a bit, but not as much as it is rumored in Rome. I heard there are a few cases of the disease that shows up with carbuncles, while most people die with dark spots on their skins and with pneumonia.[86] As to your return, although I long for it greatly, I would advise you to delay it somewhat and wait and see what your friends advise you to do. I would also urge you to put in effect the plan you had when you left from here, of visiting the holy house of Loreto.

This week Vincenzo wrote us a letter and sent a hunk of prosciutto. I would like to know how often Your Lordship hears from him. Giuseppe has made a speedy recovery and left the hospital. He will stay with his uncle in Florence for a few days. Piera is well and keeps busy weaving. She has picked a few lemons, the lowest on the trees, before the thieves could get away with them. I am told that those left on the branches are very beautiful, and so are the broad beans, which are starting to develop the fruit. I hope you will be here to pick them, when they are ready.

I send you affectionate greetings in everybody's name, and on the part of Signor Rondinelli and Signor Orsi, and I pray God to grant you all good things.

Your most devoted daughter Sister Maria Celeste
From San Matteo at Arcetri. April 16, 1633.

Sister Isabella begs you to have the enclosed message delivered by hand to the addressee, as she would like to receive an answer immediately. When he came to bless the convent, our governor asked about you and told me to send his regards.

LXXXIV

[Sent to Rome]

Most beloved Lord and Father:

I have been informed by Signor Geri of your present situation in regard with the affair you are dealing with in Rome; in short, that you are detained in the rooms of the Holy Office.[87] On the one hand, I am terribly anguished about it, thinking that you must be distraught and perhaps also very uncomfortable. On the other hand, I derive a feeling of relief from considering that this mishap has perhaps come to pass in order to bring about a speedy conclusion of the whole matter. Moreover, the kindness with which those people have treated you so far, but especially your innocence and the justice of your cause, give me ground to hope and believe in a felicitous ending, with the help of the Lord, whom I never cease to entreat, and to whom I recommend you with all my heart and in total confidence.

The only thing that remains for you to do is to be in good cheer, and try not to damage your health with continuous and excessive worrying. Address your mind to the Lord, and place your hopes in him, for he is our very loving father and never abandons those who confide in him and turn to him for help. My very dear Lord and Father, I am writing to you now because I wish you to know that I am aware of your problems and I share your distress. Perhaps this will comfort you a little. I have told no one else here, wishing these rather unpleasant facts to be my sole concern, while the pleasant and propitious events in your life I think should be shared by the whole world. Anyhow, we all are waiting for your return and look forward to enjoying your conversation and to being happy together again. And who knows? At this very moment that I am writing to you, you might already be out of danger and of all possible worry. May it please the Lord, and he be the one to bring you solace, and in his hands I leave you.

Most devoted daughter Sister Maria Celeste
From San Matteo at Arcetri. April 20, 1633.

LXXXV

[Sent to Rome]

Most illustrious and most beloved Lord and Father:

Although in your last letter you do not give any detail of your situation, perhaps because you do not want to make me participant in your suffering, I, in some other way, have learned something about it, as you will be able to gather from a letter that I wrote to you last Wednesday. And indeed in these last days I have been perturbed and bewildered, but now that you reassure me about your health, I feel much relieved.

I certainly will do what you order me to, but in the meanwhile I thank you for the generous gift of money you made to Sister Arcangela. Thank you for her and for myself too, as all her worries are also mine. We are all healthy here at the convent, thank God, but there are many rumors about the cases of the nasty disease occurring in Florence and even somewhere outside the city.[88] For this reason, I pray you, even if your affair is expedited, do not start on your return journey in such manifest danger of life, especially when you consider that your kind hosts have offered you the possibility of staying there as long as you need. Sister Luisa, together with all those mentioned above, returns your greetings in duplicate, and I pray God to grant you an abundance of grace. Please give my regards to her excellency, the lady of the house.

Most devoted daughter Sister Maria Celeste
From San Matteo at Arcetri. April 23, 1633.

LXXXVI

[Sent to Rome]

Most beloved Lord and Father:

I have seen the letter that you recently wrote to Signor Geri, who is indeed very courteous and always solicitous to give me news of you, and, although you were not well at the time of writing, now I feel reassured, and hope that you are better at present, as I am also happy to read that your affair is heading toward a speedy and satisfactory solution.[89] This week I have received a letter from her excellency, the ambassadress. She has been so kind as to inform me of your present situation, because she says, she does not believe I have received any letter from you since you went out of her house, and she does not want me to worry. I read this as a clear sign of the love that those important people have for you, a love so abundant as to extend in great measure to me, just as the said lady reassures me in her very kind letter. I replied addressing my letter to her, for I believe this to be the correct way.

There is good news about the epidemic, and it is hoped, as far as it is possible to ascertain, that it will shortly cease completely. So, God willing, it will no longer be an obstacle to your return. At this moment I am busy with the man who is here to repair, I should say to make, a still for us. This is the reason for my writing such a short note. We are all well, except Sister Luisa, who for three days has been suffering with her usual stomach pains, but not as severely as before. Giuseppe is reasonably well, and Piera quite well. Signor Rondinelli sends his greetings and will do us the favor of paying the rent money to Signor Lorenzo Bini.[90] The father confessor too sends his regards, and the same do all these nuns, particularly Sister Arcangela. May our Lord keep you safe.

Most devoted daughter Sister Maria Celeste
From San Matteo. Last day of April, 1633.

LXXXVII

[Sent to Rome]

Most beloved Lord and Father:

This morning I did not have the time to replay to your statement, that you are willing to help and come to the rescue of the
two of us but not of all the nuns in the convent. This is what you
have come to believe would be the case if you gave me the money
for Sister Arcangela's term in office. In truth, I must say that you
do not have much knowledge of the convent's customs or, better,
of our regulations, which in truth are not too well thought out.
And this is because, after she enters this, as well as any other
office, according to her rank of seniority, each nun must incur in
some expenses, and it is her responsibility to find the sum of
money necessary to carry on with her tasks, and if she does not
succeed, too bad for her. As it is often the case, these sums of
money are procured in underhanded and oblique ways (to use
your expression), and much wheeling and dealing occurs. It is
impossible to do otherwise, since a poor nun who is being made
provisioner is forced to dispose of one hundred scudi. So far I
have been able to provide almost forty scudi for Sister Arcangela,
some of which I borrowed from Sister Luisa, and the rest I took
from our income, of which only sixteen are left to be cashed for
the whole month of May.

Sister Oretta spent fifty scudi and now we are in great shortage of money and I do not know where to turn to. So, since God keeps you alive for our benefit, availing myself and making capital of this privilege, I pray Your Lordship to relieve me from this worrisome burden for the love of God, and lend me whatever money you can until next year. And at the time when we are be able to be repaid by those who owe us money, we shall return the sum to you. Now I am in a hurry and I bid you good-bye.

Your devoted daughter Sister Maria Celeste
[May 1633]

LXXXVIII

[Sent to Rome]

Most illustrious and most beloved Lord and Father:

The happiness that your last dear letter brought me was so intense, and such was the perturbation it caused in me—together with the fact that I was obliged to read it and reread it many times over to these nuns who went all in a tizzy to hear about the successful outcome of your affair—that I was taken with a terrible headache, lasting from morning until late at night, which is really something unusual for me.

I wanted you to know these details, not because I wish to reproach you for the small inconvenience I suffered, but because I would like you to be fully aware of how much I am concerned and care about what happens to you, and also of what effect it has on me, an effect which in general could be reasonably imputed to filial love, as we must expect all children to have, but which in me, I believe, has a greater strength, for I am such, I dare say, as to be advanced beyond most other children in loving and revering my dearest father, just as I see that, on your part, you love me more than most fathers love their daughters. And now let us put this matter to rest.

Endless thanks are due to the Holy Lord for the many favors he has bestowed on you, and, we may hope, he will continue to grant you in the future, for you derive most blessings from his merciful hand, as you rightly recognize. And although you attribute all mercies to the efficacy of my prayers, this is really of little merit or none at all. On the other hand, great is indeed the love with which I petition for them to the Divine Majesty, who takes my affection into consideration and grants my wishes in allowing you to prosper so. We therefore remain obliged to God, as we also are greatly indebted to all the people who favor and are helping Your Lordship, particularly those exquisite hosts of yours. I wanted to write to the excellency the lady ambassador, but I refrained myself from further annoying her as I would have, by going on and on with the same things, that is proffering my thanks and my avowals of endless obligation. Instead of writing to her, I would like you to give her my regards. And truly, my dear father, the favors you received, with the kindness and the protection of these important people, are enough to mitigate, if not to erase, all the suffering you have been going through.

I happened to come by an excellent prescription against the plague, I have made a copy of it and I am sending it to you not because I think in Rome there might be any danger of such illness, but because it is good to protect oneself from all sorts of nasty affliction. I am so short, in fact totally deprived, of the necessary ingredients, even for myself, that I cannot let you have any. Your Lordship will have to procure those that perchance are lacking from the apothecary of God's mercy. May God be with you, and together with this wish I send greetings from all of us, particularly from Sister Arcangela, and Sister Luisa too, who, at the moment, is enjoying a fairly good state of health.

Most devoted daughter Sister Maria Celeste
From San Matteo at Arcetri. May 7, 1633.

LXXXIX

[Sent to Rome]

Most beloved Lord and Father:

You must have read what intense happiness your letter of this past week brought to me. Now I can add that, as I made a copy of it before handing it back to Signor Geri for him to pass on to Vincenzo, Signor Rondinelli too read it and said he wanted to take it to Florence and show it to some friends of his, who, he assured me, would be especially pleased to hear about the details you gave us. And that is what happened, as far as I was told when he returned the letter to me. Signor Rondinelli, by the way, comes and stays in your house from time to time, but no one else does.

Piera tells me that she never goes out, except when she comes here to hear mass or on some errand. The boy at times goes to pick up the mail as far as the Bonaccorsi brothers, but nowhere else, both in order to avoid the danger of the epidemic and because he is rather weak, besides being full of the rabies he has contracted in the hospital. At present he medicates it with an ointment that I make for him. As for the rest, I see to it that he and Piera are taken well care of, as you can see from the enclosed paper where I have marked all the expenses, as well as the amount I received for the purpose. As this last sum is higher than the expenditure by several lire, I have made sure to spend the difference for Sister Arcangela's needs and mine. So now I can say we are even, and from this moment on we can make a new start. The other expenses incurred after Your Lordship's departure are: 172 scudi to Signor Lorenzo Bini for the rent of the villa; 24 scudi for the payments due four times to Vincenzo Landucci; 6, 13, and 4 scudi for the February salaries (I have receipts for all of them); 25 that I took for that matter of Sister Arcangela's, as you know; and 15 additional scudi I was forced to pay in order to wind up that blessed office of hers: the office that was brought to a close with the Lord's help and yours, because without that great push we should not have been able to come through. As a matter of fact, even the nuns were very satisfied with how it turned out. Indeed, with your help and the money we paid, we were able to cover up several mistakes, or rather misdeeds. I expect to return these last 15 scudi from both our incomes, which we ought to have been able to cash by now.

This year it was Sister Arcangela's turn to become provisioner, an office that would have given me a lot to worry about. By adducing a variety of excuses, I have persuaded Mother Superior not to assign this task to her; in exchange Sister Arcangela was chosen to look after the linen. She will have to see that the washing is done and keep track of all the towels and table cloths used in the convent.

It is especially rewarding to hear that you are in good health. I was very worried about you, considering the inconveniences you had to endure. But it pleased God to grant you full favor and to free you from all possible trouble, both of body and soul. May he be forever thanked! We hear the contagion is still out there, but they also say that only a few people are dying of it now, and there is hope it will end soon, for it has been decided to take the Madonna dell'Impruneta on a procession through Florence.[91]

The letter addressed to our former father confessor I sent on to him in Florence, for he is no longer at our convent and we now have another father, a young man thirty-five years of age, from Pieve a Santo Stefano.

I am surprised that Vincenzo never wrote to you. I am proud to have surpassed him in my diligence of writing to you regularly, although at times I too have been pressed for time. Today, for instance, I wrote this letter in four installments, because I was interrupted by various complications occurring in the pharmacy. Furthermore, for several days, I have been suffering from the usual mouth infection that gives me a persistent toothache. Now I close and send you greetings on the part of the people mentioned above, and by asking you to return those from your excellent hostess multiplied by the hundreds. I pray God to keep you healthy and favor you forever.

Your most devoted daughter Sister Maria Celeste
From San Matteo at Arcetri. May 14, 1633.

Piera received eight bushels of wheat from San Casciano. I did not try to pay for it, because I knew of some outstanding accounts between you and Ninci.

XC

[Sent to Rome]

Most beloved Lord and Father:

I never let the regular courier go by without writing to you and sending the letter to Signor Geri. He tells me that at this time you must have received my last one. As to your coming back with this courier, I could not suggest what to do with any degree of assurance on account of the current epidemic, and also in consideration of the fact that the life of the entire city is in the hands of the Very Holy Virgin. With this thought in mind, they have carried the miraculous image of the Madonna dell'Impruneta around Florence, and we understand it will remain there for three more days, and then, when it is taken back to its place, we hope we too shall be able to see it.[92] Let us wait and see what happens after that, by next Saturday we should know. In the meanwhile we can say that the procrastination is all to your advantage, and for that reason I feel less vexed by the deprivation caused by your absence.

In our neighborhood there have been two instances of the plague: two peasants were taken ill, but as of now we hear of no other occurrence and, given the case that all the well-to-do people around here have withdrawn into their villas, I take it to mean that there is no danger.[93]

I would be very grateful if, for Sister Luisa's sake, you could arrange to give our old man something to do in your studio; but first Your Lordship would have to talk to Signor Giovanni Mancini about it. We sent the papers to him some time ago but never received an answer, either from him or from anyone else to whom we had entrusted this matter.

I had a small taste of the wine that was brought to me from the two full barrels: I think it is very good. Piera tells me she has refilled them several times, and there has been no more need of it for quite a while.

Giuseppe is here waiting to take this letter with him, so I cannot write anything else, I only want to beg you not to drink to excess, as I hear you are doing.[94] I send you greeting on everyone's part and pray God to grant you true happiness.

Your most devoted daughter Sister Maria Celeste
From San Matteo. May 21, 1633.

XCI

[Sent to Rome]

Most illustrious and most beloved Lord and Father:

From the enclosed letter, written to me today by Signor Rondinelli, Your Lordship will be able to gather a good knowledge of the state of the epidemic and of the situation in Florence and in our area. Conditions being much improved now and you having brought your affairs in Rome to a conclusion, it is my hope that you will soon come home to us, who greatly yearn to have you back. So I pray you not to let yourself be delayed by the indescribable kindness of those excellent friends of yours and do not deprive us of yourself for the entire summer. You have enjoyed their hospitality long enough, and you will never be able to reciprocate the many graces and favors received from them, and which we have shared with you.

I would like you to give my usual special regards to her excellency, the lady ambassador. Furthermore I would appreciate your bringing back a small quantity of starch, as you did in the past; and remember the two pictures that I asked for a while ago.[95]

And now to the state of the orchard. As far as I understand from Piera, the broad beans have put out beautiful leaves, and have come up as high as you are, but the fruit is scanty and not so good. The same for the artichokes, which, I understand, are not as well developed as last year. Nonetheless there is enough for the house, for us, and a small quantity to be sent to Vincenzo and Signor Geri.

The orange trees have not put out a great deal of flowers so far, for they were greatly damaged by the cold and wind that raged in the past several days. Now and then Piera picks up the flowers that fall down and distills them. The lemons are ripe and in urgent need for you to come and pick them; those few that from time to time fall to the ground are beautiful and very juicy. This is as much as the work in the shop allows me to write for the moment, because Sister Luisa and another of my friends are kept under medical observation, and, as a consequence, I am the only one in the apothecary to do the work. I send you affectionate greetings on the part of the usual nuns, of Sister Barbara and Sister Prudenza too, and I pray our Lord to look after you.

Your most devoted daughter Sister Maria Celeste
From San Matteo. May 28, 1633.

XCII

[Sent to Rome]

Most beloved Lord and Father:

In my last letter I gave you an auspicious report on the epidemic (thanks to God and the Blessed Madonna, whose miracle must be acknowledged), and now I will give you even better news. I heard that yesterday nobody died and only two people were taken to the Lazzaretto.[96] They were ill of other diseases and were sent there because the hospitals cannot take any more. patients, or only a limited number. It is rumored that there are still some cases of the epidemic in the countryside toward Rovezzano, but very few. With good precautions, and the warm weather coming on very strong now, it is hoped that the disease will totally disappear in a very short time.

Around here there are no signs of the plague whatsoever. The families that suffered at the beginning of the epidemic were the Grazzinis, who worked for the Lanfredinis, and the Farciglis, who lived half way down the hill. The latter was a family divided into two or three houses. I do not know whom they worked for, all I know is that all of them died. This is all the information that with a great deal of patience, I have been able to gather for you, in the hope to spur you on the way home, provided you have been able to bring your business to a conclusion. Surely your absence has been far too long already, and I would not want you to delay your return until the fall in any way, as I fear you might do, if you keep putting it off.[97] All the more so, as, I understand, you are now free, and, besides, very pleasantly entertained. I am certainly glad for this, but, at the same time, I am sorry to learn that your pains give you no respite, although it seems to me that the pleasure you enjoy in drinking such excellent wines must necessarily be balanced by some suffering, and that perhaps, by abstaining from drinking more, you would be offsetting any greater damage you might receive from indulging too much.

Pressed as I was for time, I did not manage to tell you in my last letter that on its return from Florence, the image of the holy Madonna dell'Impruneta came by our church. This visit was indeed an exceptional grace for us, because, as the procession was advancing slowly on the valley on its way back to the original church, it was made to deviate on purpose in order to come here to us, and then it had to go down again, along the way you know so well. To think that the tabernacle alone, with all those decorations, weighs seven hundred pounds! And because it could not pass through our gate, we had to brake down the wall of the courtyard and then raise the church door, which we did with great speed and eagerness for the occasion.

After insistently sending someone to ask the return of two scudi, Sister Arcangela of San Giorgio[98] now writes to me and makes a great fuss over the death of her sister Sibilla. She begs me to ask you, as I am doing, to have a mass celebrated for her sister's soul over the alter of Saint Gregory. She would like to be reassured of this and have some peace of mind about it: she promises to pray for you tirelessly.

Just now, thinking of Saint Gregory, I remembered that you never told me if you received that prescription for the plague I sent you some time ago. It seems strange to me for surely I sent you an excellent remedy indeed, and I wonder whether it went lost. And now I close and send you affectionate greetings, also on the part of the usual nuns, and pray our Lord to grant you his holy grace.

Most devoted daughter Sister Maria Celeste
From San Matteo at Arcetri. June 4, 1633.

XCIII

[Sent to Rome]

Most beloved Lord and Father:

In my last letter I wrote that the casualties of the epidemic had considerably decreased. Regrettably, I cannot give you the same assurances now, because in the last few days, with a change in the weather and a much cooler season than it is customary for this time of the year, the contagion has gained strength and every day we hear about new houses being locked up.[99] However, the number of deaths is not high, not surpassing, it seems, seven or eight casualties per day, and the same number of people taken ill. This being the situation at present, I suppose you could come by way of Siena, as already planned, provided, however, that your business for the current month is completed, because, as I understand from Signor Rondinelli, it will not be safe to cross the Roman countryside until the fall, and I would not like you to have to remain in Rome for such a long time. So please expedite your departure as much as you can, as I hope you will be able to do with God's help and with the aid of the ambassador, who, one could easily see, was tireless in helping and favoring you in every way he could. And in truth, my dear Lord and Father, if, on the one hand, the Almighty God has humiliated and inflicted pain on you, on the other hand, he has lifted you up and protected you. For indeed, he has especially graced you, letting you come safely through all the discomforts encountered on your journey and through the troubling vicissitudes that followed. May it be God's pleasure to allow us to be grateful for his many benefices, and may he protect you and keep you safe to the very end. For this I pray him from the bottom of my heart and comment myself to you a thousandfold, together with my usual friends.

Most devoted daughter Sister Maria Celeste
From San Matteo at Arcetri, June 11, 1633.

XCIV

[Sent to Rome]

Most beloved Lord and Father:

When I wrote you an account of the epidemic in our area, almost all danger had already disappeared. Many days, in fact weeks, had gone by with no new cases of the disease. And, as I added then, great confidence was inspired by the fact that all the well-to-do people around here remained in their villas—where they still are—and even more by the fact that in Florence itself the pestilence seemed to have decreased to the point that it was hoped it would soon disappear all together. Given such reassurances, I began to urge and solicit your return. However, in the last letter I wrote, and that was when the situation was beginning to turn for the worse, I changed my tune, so to speak. And that is because, as much as I long to see you at the earliest, nonetheless I care far more for your safety and continued well-being, and I look at your chance of remaining in Rome longer than you and I had counted on as God's special grace. And if, on the one hand, I am persuaded that being detained there in tender hooks must be vexing for you, on the other hand I realize that a greater inconvenience might be finding yourself in the perilous situation that exists here, for the danger of the plague is still around and perhaps on the increase. This much I infer from an order that the convent has received from the officers of public health, that two nuns in turn must pray the Divine Majesty for forty days without interruption for the liberation of this scourge. From the same officers we have received a contribution of twenty-five scudi, and today makes the fourth day of prayer.

I told Sister Arcangela Landucci that you will carry out the errand that she asked for and she thanks you no end.

In giving you news about your home, I will start from the dovecote. The doves have been breeding since the end of Lent. The first pair of newborns were eaten by some animal during the night. Piera found the hatching dove lying on a beam without entrails and half eaten, so she thought the culprit must have been some bird of prey. The other doves were frightened and flew away, but Piera kept putting out the feed for them, so they came back and started breeding again. At present two doves are hatching.

The orange trees have grown a few flowers, and Piera has distilled the petals and got about two quarts of orange water. As to the capers, they will be taken care of when the time comes. The lettuce that you ordered to be planted never took hold, so in its place Piera planted beans. She tells me that they are fine. As to the chickpeas, they would be fine too, but it seems that the hares have already started to eat them up. As to the broad beans, the crop was sufficient to let some of it dry, while the stalks are being given to the mule to eat. Your lady mule, by the way, is behaving in a very haughty manner and does not want to carry anyone any longer. A couple of times she bounced poor Geppo off the saddle into a somersault, but she did it gently and he was not hurt. When he had to go out a few days ago, Ascanio—the brother of Geppo's sister-in-law—asked for the mule, but when he was near Porta al Prato, he was forced to turn around and come back because he could not master the strength to prevail on the animal's obstinacy and make her go any further. It seems that in absence of her master, the mule does not want to be ridden by anyone but him.

Going back to the orchard, the vines are showing up very nicely. I wonder whether they will continue to do so, after the affront of being tended to by Piera's hands instead of yours. The artichokes were not many, just enough for eating and some for preserving. Everything in the cellar is fine; the wine keeps very well. As far as the pantry goes, it is I who usually dispense the food to the servants, except when Signor Rondinelli is in and takes care of it. As a matter of fact, one morning this week, he was so thoughtful as to ask us to lunch with him in the convent parlor. This is all the news that I seem to be able to give you for the time being.

Since in Rome there are so many good composers, Sister Achilla would like you to find some beautiful music to play on the organ. Sister Luisa is interested to know if you have seen Giovanni Mancini, the merchant, on account of that business about our old man, while Sister Isabella asks whether the letter she sent for Signor Francesco Cavalcanti was delivered, because she would like to find out from him if a brother of hers who lives there is dead or alive. Now I close, so that I will have something left to say next time I write. But I just remembered that I have to give you greetings on the part of Sister Barbara. She asked me to tell you exactly this: she no longer goes out, except to go to church by the nearest exit, in order to deck it out and tidy up. The other friends say hello, and I pray the Holy God to give you all real wealth.

Most devoted daughter Sister Maria Celeste
From San Matteo. June 18, 1633.

XCV

[Sent to Rome]

Most beloved Lord and Father:

May the Lord be thanked, for I hear that you have begun to arrange your departure from Rome. I have greatly longed for this moment not only because I wish to see you but also because now that your business is over and done with, you will finally be able after so many months to live in peace and tranquillity. So we can bless all past tribulations, for they are coming to an end with the favorable outcome that you seem to be hoping for.

I am happy that Your Lordship is going to Siena and thus be avoiding the dangers of the plague, which, anyhow, is thought to be on the wane at the moment, and also because I expect you will enjoy a most rewarding stay, judging from the courteous and insistent invitation you have received from that archbishop. I pray you, then, do come back at your own pace and, since you had to travel during the two harshest seasons of the year, try to make your move as comfortable as possible. Please, keep sending news of yourself as often as you can, just as you have done all along during this absence. I thank you for this, which is indeed the greatest gift I could have received. With this note I thought of sending a letter for the lady ambassador (to whom I feel so very much obliged for the love of you), but I do not know whether you will still be there when it arrives. So I have decided to put it off until next week, or better until you advise me whether I ought to send it or not. As to the matter of our old man, we shall talk about it when you are here, God willing, for I pray him to guard and keep you safe all throughout this journey. Warmest greetings, on the part of the usual friends as well.

Your most devoted daughter Sister Maria Celeste
From San Matteo at Arcetri. June 25, 1633.

XCVI

[Sent to Rome]

Most illustrious and beloved Lord and Father:

Hearing about the decision that in the end was made about your book, and about yourself, has pierced my soul with extreme sorrow; all the more so as the news of this misfortune has arrived suddenly and against our expectations. I found this out from Signor Geri. I insisted that he should tell me about it, because this week I received no letters from you and I could not calm myself down, having almost a premonition of what happened. My dearest Lord and Father, now is the time, more than ever before, to avail yourself of the wisdom that God has granted you, and to bear these blows with the fortitude that religion, your profession, and your age demand. And since from much experience you have acquired full knowledge of how fallacious and unstable are all the things of this ugly world of ours, you ought not to make a great deal out of these storms, but rather hope that they will soon abate and change into something very much to your satisfaction.

I say this prompted by my own desire, and also by what the clemency shown toward you by his Holiness seems to promise, for he has chosen such a charming place for your prison. It seems then that we may hope even for a commutation of your jail sentence into something more consonant to your wishes and ours. May God allow this to happen, if it is for the best. In the

meantime I pray you, do not fail to comfort me with your letters, and give me details of your condition, both of body and
more important, of your soul. Now I will stop writing, but I can
assure you I will always be with you in my thoughts and
prayers, for I shall entreat the Divine Majesty to grant you alle-
viation of your pain and true serenity

Most devoted daughter Sister Maria Celeste
From San Matteo at Arcetri. July 2, 1633

XCVII

[Sent to Siena]

Most illustrious and most beloved Lord and Father:

The letter that you wrote from Siena (in which you say you are comfortable and in good health) brought me great joy, and to Sister Arcangela too. There is no need for me to labor trying to make my words persuasive, because you can penetrate my thoughts better than I can explain them. Still, I would like to be able to describe to you the jubilation and the rejoicing that these sisters and mothers went through at hearing about your happy return. It was something extraordinary! When they heard the news, mother the abbess, and many other sisters, started to run toward me with open arms, all the while crying aloud, out of happiness for you and tenderness toward me. This event has tied me to them with a strong bond of affection for I understood how deeply they feel towards you and us.

Furthermore, reading that you are the guest of a man as well disposed and considerate as monsignor the archbishop doubles my pleasure and satisfaction, although this turn of events may come out against our own interest, for such pleasant company may easily detain you there longer than we would wish. But since the danger of the plague here is not over yet, I am pleased by your delay and by your decision to wait to be reassured by your dearest friends, who will keep you informed about the real situation, if not with more love, at least with more certainty than we could.

Meanwhile, I think it would be better to take a profit from some of the wine in your cellar, at least from one barrel, because, although it keeps rather well for the time being, I am afraid that, with the warm weather coming, it might give us a surprise. The barrel that you had began to tap, and from which now the servants drink, has already started to turn sour. You may want to tell us what we ought to do, since I do not have much knowledge in these matters. At the same time, I cannot help considering that since you were provided for a whole year and have been away for six months now, there is good reason to expect that there will be some wine left over, even in the event that you come back in a few days.

Leaving this subject aside and going back to what matters to me most, I really would like to know how it can be that your affair has ended satisfactorily for both you and for your adversaries, as you mentioned in the letter before the last from Rome. Do explain this to me at your convenience and when you are well rested, for I will be glad to wait a little longer for you to persuade me of this contradiction.

Signor Geri came here one morning when it was feared that you might be in a tight spot, and together with Signor Aggiunti, carried out that errand in your home which, he later told me, he had advised you about. It seemed to me something well done and a necessary precaution if we wanted to avoid the complications that might have followed, so I could not deny him the keys and the possibility to get on with it, chiefly as I realized in what a rush he was to act in your interest.[100]

I wrote to the lady ambassador last Saturday with all the consideration and love that I could master, and, if I receive an answer, Your Lordship will be informed. Now I stop writing because I am falling to sleep, as it is the third hour of the night.[101] So you will excuse me if I have been writing a lot of nonsense. I return your greetings in duplicate from all the people mentioned above, especially from Piera and Geppo who are jumping for happiness at the news of your return, and I pray the blessed Lord to grant you his holy grace.

Most devoted daughter Sister Maria Celeste
From San Matteo at Arcetri. July 13, 1633.

XCVIII

[Sent to Siena]

Most illustrious and most beloved Lord and Father:

It was with great pleasure that I read the letter that you sent to Signor Mario,[102] for it made me realize that you are in a state of inner peace. What you say calms me too and puts my mind almost entirely to rest; but not quite, because you are far away and I do not know when I will be able to see you. This goes to show that nothing in this world can give us total peace and contentment. When you were in Rome, I used to turn this thought in my mind: once he leaves Rome, by the grace of God, and goes to Siena, I will be happy, for I then will be able to say that he is almost at home. Now that you are at Siena, I am not satisfied, because I long to have you near me. But anyway, let us thank God for the great blessings with which he has graced us so far. We must be grateful to him, and perchance move and dispose him to granting us more in the future, as I hope he will do in his mercy. As to myself, I take into greater account this grace than any other, which is his having kept you safe and sound all throughout your past tribulations.

I do not have time to say more at present. I will write to a great length when I answer your next letter, which must arrive soon; I will then give you a detailed account of what has happened in your house. I send you greetings from all of us, as usual, and from

Signor Rondinelli, who is so affectionate toward us; and I pray God to give you solace.

Most devoted daughter Sister Maria Celeste
From San Matteo at Arcetri. July 16, 1633.

XCIX

[Sent to Siena]

Most illustrious and most beloved Lord and Father:

Signor Geri could not show me the letter addressed to him because he had to leave it with the grand duke, but he promised to let me read it as soon as possible.

In the meanwhile I am satisfied with the one you wrote to me, for I understand that you are in good health, comfortable and pleased. I thank God for it, because, as I said before I recognize that your safety was granted as a special grace.

Yesterday morning I had a small quantity of your wine brought to me for tasting. One barrel is very good, the other has a bad color, and I do not like the taste either, for it seems about to turn. This evening I will ask Signor Rondinelli to taste it too. He will be at the villa on Saturday as usual, and will then be able to judge better than I can whether the wine is safe to drink, because as far as the taste goes, it is not too unpleasant. I will let you know, so you can advise us on what to do in case his report is in the negative. The white wine that is in the flasks is already strong, and we think it will make an exquisite vinegar. The wine in the demijohn has only a bit of fire and so we decided to drink it before it turns completely into vinegar. This was not Piera's fault because she checked it many times, making sure that the flasks were always full.

The capers have been attended to, and a good amount is now preserved—which takes care of all the capers grown in your orchard—for Piera tells me that you are very fond of them. There has been no flour in the house for several days. I told the boy to buy bread at the shop: in this hot weather one cannot bake a big quantity of bread because it grows moldy and stale immediately, and it does not pay to warm the haven for a few loaves.

In my next letter I shall give you a detailed account of what was paid out day by day. At the moment I have no energy left. As it is usual with me at this season of the year, I feel so weak that I hardly have any strength to push the pen on the paper, as it were. So I send you warm greetings, also on the part of all the mothers. One hour feels like a year to them, so great is their desire to see you again. May the Lord keep you safe.

Most devoted daughter Sister Maria Celeste
From San Matteo at Arcetri. July 23, 1633.

C

[Sent to Siena]

Most illustrious and most beloved Lord and Father:

I read the letter you addressed to Signor Geri with special interest and satisfaction, especially for the things written in the first part. As to the third section, which has to do with the purchase of a small house that, as I surmised, Signor Geri would very much like Vincenzo to buy—with your help—I have decided that I too shall express an opinion. I wouldn't want to be presumptuous and interfere in matters which do not concern me; nonetheless, because I have any interest of yours to my heart, no matter how small, I would suggest, as matter of fact I would urge you, to yield to Geri's wishes, provided you are now in the financial position to do so. I would like you to contribute to this purchase, if not totally, at least in part, not as much for Vincenzo's sake, but rather to keep Signor Geri in that friendly disposition in which he proved to be toward you on several occasions in the past, when he showed great affection for you and, as far as I could tell, did his best to defend your interests. So giving him a sign of gratitude, if you can do it without much bother to yourself, would be something well considered. I know that you understand these things and can take care of them infinitely better than I could. Perhaps I do not know what I am talking about; what I know is that I speak out of true affection for you.

The servant who was in Rome with you came here yesterday morning, as he was asked to do by Sir Giulio Ninci. It seems strange to me that he had no letter to deliver. Even so, I was persuaded by the explanation he gave that you did not know that he would come by. Now that you are without a servant, our Geppo cannot keep still and would like to come to you by any manner or means, if he were granted permission. That would please me too. So let us know how you feel about it and then I would see to it that he travels with a good escort, while Signor Geri, I believe, could arrange for him to obtain a passport. I would also like to know how much straw we should buy. Piera is afraid the mule will starve to death, as the fodder never seems enough, and, as it is, the animal is more difficult to please than she ought to be.

Since the last time I sent you an account of the money used for your household, these have been the expenditures, all written down on the enclosed paper. Marked are also the amounts paid to Vincenzo Landucci each month. I have receipts for everything except for these last payments, because at the time—and the situation continues to this day—he was locked up in his house with his small children. It is rumored that his wife died of the plague. She can really be said to have gone to her rest by escaping her tribulations, poor woman. He sent someone to collect the six scudi due to him, for the love of God, he entreated, for he had nothing to eat and it was already the end of the month. He promised to send the receipts as soon as he is declared out of danger; and I will make sure that he does, at least before I fork out the other money, unless you are here by that time, but I doubt that you will be, considered the excessive heat that we are made to suffer this summer.

In the orchard the lemons were all falling down, so those few that were left have been sold, and the two lire made from the sale I spent to have three masses sung for Your Lordship, as per my intention. I wrote to the lady ambassador as you ordered me to do and consigned the letter to Signor Geri, but I have received no reply. Now I am in doubt whether it would be a good idea to write to her again to wonder whether my letter or hers went astray. And, finally, I send you my warmest greetings and pray the Lord to keep you safe and sound.

Most devoted daughter Sister Maria Celeste
From San Matteo at Arcetri. July 24, 1633.

CI

[Sent to Siena]

Most beloved Lord and Father:

I am surprised to read that a regular courier went by without delivering any mail from me, for I never stopped writing and forwarding my letters to Signor Geri. Last week I wrote twice, once on Saturday and again on Monday. Perhaps by now you have received both letters and are appraised about everything that has been going on in your house, just as you wanted.

The report on the wine was incomplete; the only thing missing was Signor Rondinelli's opinion on the state of the barrels. On his advice, because the dregs in one barrel looked very mucky, we decanted the wine into another barrel. Now we shall wait for a few days, and if the wine does not improve, we will try to arrange a sale before it is totally spoiled. This is the barrel I warned you about; the other is keeping very well.

I have not forgotten to prepare the aloe for Your Lordship. I have given it the rose water seven times, but at the moment the mixture is not sufficiently dry and cannot be shaped into pills. I am therefore sending a number of those made for our shop, which are also prepared with aloe washed up with rose water, but only once. Nonetheless I do not think that they will hurt you just this time, since they have been sweetened somewhat.

As to whether Landucci is grieving for the death of his wife, I am not in a position to say. I know nothing about it except what Giuseppe told me the day he went to his house with Signor Rondinelli to pay the six scudi, and that was on the 18th of this month. Geppo said that he placed the money on the doorstep and that he saw Vincenzo inside the house, away from the door, that he looked very depressed, with a deadly expression on his face, and that around him were his little children, a boy and a girl, which is just how many he has left alive.

I am glad that you are keeping in good health and I beg you to take care of yourself and be moderate in drinking, for it is so bad for you. I am afraid that this terrible heat and the pleasant company you enjoy may be the reason for you to go overboard, thus running the risk of getting ill and postponing your return to Florence again. That is against all our wishes.

This week, our Signora Giulia, Sister Luisa's mother and Signor Corso's sister, came face to face with death but got through against all expectations, although she is eighty-five years old and seemed so far gone as to be about to be given extreme unction. Now she is out of danger, has no fever, and returns your regards a thousandfold. The same do all my friends. May the Lord grant you his holy grace.

Most devoted daughter Sister Maria Celeste
From San Matteo at Arcetri. July 28, 1633.

CII

[Sent to Siena]

Most beloved Lord and Father:

I am jotting down these few lines because I do not wish to disobey your order not to let one week go by without writing to you.

With regard to the wine that was decanted, it seems to have improved in color. Piera does not dislike drinking it and will do so as the days go by. A way was found to exchange three barrels of it as table wine.[103] The blacksmith will get two barrels, a worker from Ambra half a barrel, and the man who works on Beni's farm will get the other half. And because I do not want any to go to waist, we shall try to place still another barrel. What is left, and that is a little more than a barrel, your servants will be very happy to drink themselves, and Sister Arcangela will not take too much persuading to help them out.

Two pairs of pigeons were born in the dovecote. They are waiting for you to come and give them the death sentence. The lemons promise well for the time being, but the bitter and the sweet oranges have put out only a few flowers, and, from these, even fewer fruit are coming out; still, it is something.

The loafs of bread your people buy for eight quattrini are white and big. Soon they will get the straw for the mule. As to the hay, it cannot be counted on because this season there was hardly any grass at all, and, besides, Piera tells me, your lady mule is not too partial to it. You will remember that last year she used the straw to make her bed with so that she could sleep in greater comfort. Recently she has grown a bit of a bother in her mouth and her stomach is so delicate that, they say, cool drinks hurt her. All this fuss has created problems for Piera, but fortunately the animal is doing better now.

You did well to open the letter addressed to the kind lady ambassador. As soon as the roads are viable again, I would like to find a way to send her some trinket to go with the crystal. Signor Geri has not yet arrived. So, for the time being, there is nothing more I can add, except to say that I read with great pleasure the description you gave in your last letter of the considerate and respectful way you are treated in that town. And now I greet you most dearly and pray God to keep you safe.

Your devoted daughter Sister Maria Celeste
From San Matteo. August 3, 1633.

CIII

[Sent to Siena]

Most beloved Lord and Father:

Yesterday morning Signor Geri came to speak to me about the purchase of the small house, and, as far as I have been able to understand, he does not expect anything from it except to be of use and benefit to Vincenzo, as would be the case if the deal were brought to a close. In fact, it would enlarge and improve Vincenzo's home, which seems to be quite cramped, especially in the event his family grows, without considering that the room above the tank, he says, is not fit to be lived in. When I asked him whether he was thinking of residing in the house with Vincenzo, Signor Geri said that even if he wanted to, he could not, and that he must find a more comfortable house near the ducal palace, because the house on the Costa is unsuitable and too much out of the way, both for him and for the people who go to see him all day long. Having ascertained this point, I conclude that Signor Geri would like you to buy the house outright, which in no way would cost more than 300 scudi, he tells me. I told him that it did not seem possible or fair to burden you with such an obligation, especially since you are probably short of money now, after so many exceptional expenditures, and I added that, since you always try to help them every way you can, we could propose and ask you to contribute half the sum, if it is possible for you at this point, and that perhaps Signor Geri himself could advance the other half, until the time when Vincenzo will be in a position to return the money to him. To this Signor Geri agreed very quickly and with much courtesy. Then he went on to explain that, in your absence, he has loaned Vincenzo other sums; nonetheless, he would be glad to take the trouble to loan him these 150 scudi as well so that Vincenzo would not miss this exceptional opportunity. This is what we agreed to propose to you, and this is what I am doing now. It is up to you to choose, for you know better than me how far you can stretch your resources. I would only add that getting my nose in this business has caused me no small distress, first of all because in general I do not wish to disturb your peace, as you asked me not to, and then, because at present you do not seem to be inclined to any new purchase, and therefore I fear I have been a bother to you. On the other hand, to ignore Signor Geri who is petitioning you for your own son and who shows so much concern for you and for all your family does not seem laudable to me. Please answer this question as soon as possible and take me out of this uncertainty.

You could also advise me what was the effect of the pills I sent to you, and whether you want me to send you more of the same, because, for the time being, I cannot use the aloe that is in preparation for new ones. Sister Giulia returns your greetings. She says she is looking forward not to the white wine you promised her but to your very self. Signor Rondinelli does the same. I always make sure to share your letters with him, whenever I think appropriate to do so. And now I commend myself to you, and pray God for your happiness.

Most devoted daughter Sister Maria Celeste
From San Matteo ar Arcetri. August 6, 1633.

CIV

[Sent to Siena]

Most beloved Lord and Father:

Once you wrote that my letters often arrive by twos. Then, not to repeat the same expression, I will say that your last mail arrived like the clogged friars, who not only go around in pairs but with a great deal of clatter as well. This is because your last letter caused in me a turmoil of happiness, when I read that the appeal I made, or better the deal I recommended in name of Signor Geri and Vincenzo, has been undersigned by you with more promptness and generosity than I had asked for. So, I infer, your peace was not disturbed by my insistence, which is what matters to me most, and now I have reason to rejoice and offer my thanks.

As far as your return is concerned, God knows how much I long for it. Even so, if you gather that, on leaving Siena, you would be made to stay in some place here other than your own home, then I would advise you, for your well-being and reputation, to remain a little longer where you are at present. For you seem to be in a paradise of delights, especially for the very pleasant company of this illustrious monsignor, the archbishop. Later, you will be able to come to your humble abode, which is lamenting for your long absence, the barrels especially. They are groaning a lot, jealous as they are of the praises you sing of the wine of those valleys over there; one of them vindictively has tried to spoil the wine, or the wine to spoil the barrel, as I reported to you. Another barrel would have done the same, if Signor Rondinelli's shrewdness and diligence had not prevented it, by procuring the appropriate remedy, that is, by arranging for the wine to be sold. And so it was, to the keeper of the inn, with the intermediary of Matteo the shopkeeper. Today the wine is being poured into flasks and two loads will be sent away. Signor Rondinelli is supervising the operation. From the deal we will get eight scudi. What is left will be kept in flasks for the family and for the two of us here, for we are willing and ready to do our part of the drinking. We hurried to arrive at this solution before the wine played us another trick, forcing us to throw it away.

Signor Rondinelli says that the reason of this mishap is that the wine was not decanted out of the first barrel before the beginning of the hot season, which is something I knew nothing about, for I lack all expertise in this field.

In the orchard the vines were not very promising and besides two fierce hailstorms finished them off. A quantity of the July grapes was picked before the thieves could get to them, and in fact, finding nothing else to plunder, they got away with a few apples. On the day of San Lorenzo the weather was horrible around here; the wind was very strong and caused a lot of damage. Some damage occurred in your place too: a good part of the roof, on the side of Signor Chellini's property, was blown off, and one of the big pots where the orange trees are planted was shattered. The tree has been transplanted into the ground, and you will let us know whether your servants should buy a new pot and move the tree into it again. We told Signor Bini about the roof and he promised to have it repaired.

There are practically no other fruits. There is not a single plum and those few pears that your trees produced were harvested by the wind. The broad beams have come up beautifully, Piera says; they will make five bushels and are quite good. After that, only some beans remain.

What would be left to write about is that question you raised about being or not being idle; but I am keeping it for a time when I am not so sleepy, because now it is the third hour of the night.[104] I send you greetings from all the people mentioned, and furthermore from Doctor Ronconi who is so thoughtful and always inquires about you, when he is here. May the Lord God keep you safe.

Most devoted daughter Sister Maria Celeste
From San Matteo. August 13, 1633.

CV

[Sent to Siena]

Most beloved Lord and Father:

When in my letter I discussed the alternative of your moving to a place near here or remaining at Siena a while longer, I knew about the petition you had presented to the ambassador but nothing about the reply. I have heard about it afterwards from Signor Geri. He arrived here last Tuesday, when I had already written to you, enclosing the recipe for the pills, which you must have received by now. The reason for writing to you in that way was the information I had gathered in my talks with Signor Rondinelli. I must say that he has been a real refuge to me in this period. As a man of the world and a very practical one, he has frequently assuaged my fears by explaining how matters were likely to turn out, while I imagined things would be more rushed than in fact they have been. Among other matters, I learned that in Florence it was rumored that you were about to leave Siena and would be moved to the Charter House: something that none of our friends would wish for you. Among the explanations Signor Rondinelli gave about your situation, one in particular—which was later brought forward by the ambassador himself, as I heard—was that, by soliciting your return too soon, you would get a negative reply, and then a longer stretch of time would have to go by before you could advance a new petition. So, fearing that this would be the result, when I read that you were urging your return, I was moved to write to you in the way I did.

If I do not make a great demonstration of my desire to see you, it is because I do not want to add to your problems and worries. But in fact, in the past few days, I have been daydreaming a lot. I was thinking to myself that perhaps, after waiting two months for the pardon in vain, I ought to turn to the lady ambassador and ask her to petition for you through his Holiness's sister-in-law. I know these are plans without foundation. Nonetheless, I would not consider it impossible for the prayers of a loving daughter to achieve what the favor of great personages cannot. I was wrapped up in these thoughts, when I read in one of your letters that one more reason for you to wish your return was to see me happy with the gift I am certain to receive. I cannot tell you how angry this statement of yours made me, but of an anger of the kind to which the blessed king David exhorts us in that psalm that says: *irascimini et nolite peccare*. And the reason is that you seem inclined to believe that I would be happier for the sight of the present than for the sight of you. This is so far from the truth as light is from darkness. Perhaps I did not understand the correct meaning of your words, and so I try to keep calm, because otherwise I do not know what I would say or do. Enough.

See if you can manage to get back to your humble abode, which no longer wants to remain empty and disconsolate, especially now that the time has come to fill the barrels again. As a punishment for spoiling the wine, the casks have been moved to the loggia and there, on the sentence of the most expert drinkers in the land, have had their bottoms knocked out. Those men pointed out a considerable fault of yours, and that is your habit of never breaking their base open, so now the casks can no longer stand it, they say, and are much the worse for it.

Of the eight scudi we got from the sale of the wine, I paid out three for six bushels of wheat, so, as soon as it gets colder, Piera can start making bread again. She sends her regards and says that if one could weigh her desire of seeing you and yours of coming home, her side of the scales would certainly go down, while your side would rise to the heavens. I will not mention how eager Geppo is for your return. This week Signor Rondinelli paid the seven scudi to Vincenzo Landucci and received two receipts, one for last month and the other for the current one. I hear Landucci and his children are fine, but I do not know how he manages to take care of them, having no way of checking on him. I am sending more pills made with the same paste as before, together with the warmest greetings from the usual friends and from Signor Rondinelli. May our Lord look after you.

Most devoted daughter Sister Maria Celeste
From San Matteo at Arcetri. August 20, 1633.

CVI

[Sent to Siena]

Most beloved Lord and Father:

I live in the hope that Your Lordship may be granted the desired pardon at the condition you tell me about. I cannot wait to hear what the result will be, so I beg you, let me know immediately, even if you get a negative answer. Still, I want to hope for the best.

I have some news: with the death of Signor Benedetto Parenti, on Wednesday last, our convent has inherited a farm at the Ambrogiana and our attorney went to take possession of it the same day.[105] We have heard many people say that it is worth more than five thousand scudi. They also say that this year the property has produced a harvest of 16 moggia[106] of wheat, and that there will also be 50 barrels of wine and 70 sacks of millet. So the circumstances of our convent are going to be ameliorated somewhat.

The day before receiving your letter, Sir Ceseri borrowed the mule to go to Fiesole and, according to Geppo, brought her back in the evening unshod and in a pitiful state all together. So I said that, if Sir Ceseri comes back to ask for the mule again, Geppo should tell him no, as politely as possible, with the excuse that the animal is not well and that you do not want her to get scratched or hurt in any way.

For several weeks now, Piera has had little to do around the house, and, since I understand that there is a great abundance of good linen where you are, I thought that, if it is true, you may want to buy a small quantity of it. If the linen is thin, it could be used to make hand towels, pillowcases, and such. I would also like you to provide me with a bit of saffron for the shop, for it is one of the ingredients in the preparation of papal pills, as you had the occasion to see.

I am not feeling very well, so I do not quite know what I am writing down. Please excuse me and wish me well. Adieu, and may God be the one to give you every consolation.

Your devoted daughter Sister Maria Celeste
From San Matteo at Arcetri. August 27, 1633.

CVII

[Sent to Siena]

Most beloved Lord and Father:

I am delighted to hear you mention a trip to the countryside. I mean to say that I am pleased for you, because I know how much you must welcome it, but I am sorry for us, for I can see that you will postpone your return even further. But let that be as it may: as long as God keeps you healthy and in good cheer, everything else will be tolerable; in fact it becomes good and pleasurable to me as well, for I hope that God Almighty, in his wisdom and mercy, will one day draw a great reward from your tribulations and ours.

The mishap with the wine was unfortunate for you but, I am about to say, was even worse for us. As we wanted you to find the barrels intact, we did not drink even a drop; and we had very little of the wine that was in the cask you left open, because it started to turn sour very soon, and we did not like it any longer. In the meanwhile, from waiting too long, even the small quantity of white wine left had turned into vinegar. In the house, there are still six bottles of the wine that was sold, which is quite passable for the servants. There is also some of the wine that went totally bad and had to be thrown away, but I do not want the servants to drink it. So, until the new season, they will have to buy wine in the flasks. I shall ask Signor Rondinelli to tell Geppo where to go to get some that is passable.

We bought a supply of three loads of excellent straw for the mule and paid seven lire and four crazie per load. This year there was no hay; furthermore, the dear beast does not go for this kind of feed.

I sent Geppo to pick up the clock some time ago, but the repairman refused to give it to him saying that he would rather wait for you. Yesterday I sent the boy again to tell him that we wanted the clock anyway, and the man made the excuse that he had to look at it and told Geppo to come back another day. This will be done, but if he does not want to give the clock back next time either, I will order the boy to go and fetch it together with Signor Rondinelli.

Dear father, I would like you to know that I am as stupid as a buffalo, a bigger one than any of those that roam around in the plains of Maremma. When I read that you intended to send six buffalo eggs, I really believe that they were eggs and I planned to make a big omelet. I went to Sister Luisa to express my happy expectation of that dish and she burst out laughing.[107] Tomorrow morning, which is Sunday, the boy will go to San Casciano to pick up the saddlebags you ordered. In the meanwhile I thank you for all the things you say you are going to send to us.

When you come back, you will no longer find Signor Donato Gherardini, the rector of Santa Margherita a Montici, brother of our Sister Lisabetta, because he died two days ago, and we still do not know who will succeed him.

Sister Polissena would like to find out if Signor Emilio Piccolomini was involved in the riots that are rumored to have occurred in your part of the world. He is the son of Captain Carlo, who was the husband of one of Sister Polissena's nieces. Sister Polissena would like to make certain of a few facts, so she may pray for him in a manner more consonant with the truth, because many of the rumors that are going around cannot be believed, for they sound a lot like old folks' tales.

The two letters that you sent in the last pouch have been delivered. There is nothing else to report except that when I receive a letter from you, as soon as I have read it, I start longing for the next courier to arrive so that I can have another one to read, especially now that I am waiting for some news to arrive from Rome.

Mother Superior—that is the abbess—Signor Rondinelli, and all the other nuns return your greetings in duplicate, and I pray the Holy God to give you an abundance of heavenly grace.

Your devoted daughter Sister Maria Celeste
From San Matteo at Arcetri. September 3, 1633.

CVIII

[Sent to Siena]

Most beloved Lord and Father:

Thursday night—and Friday too—I became so anxious about not receiving any news from you that I kept awake until late into the night, not knowing what might be the cause of your silence. And then, when your letter arrived and I read that monsignor the archbishop was aware of my blunder, I could not help feeling ashamed, while, on the other hand, I am pleased to have given you reason to be amused and laugh, and this is the reason why I write a lot of nonsense at times.

Mother Vinta was much heartened by the assurance you gave about her nephew. And when she heard what that great gentleman, the archbishop, said about being charitable, she became very agitated and declared that not only Signor Emilio but his mother too, Signora Elisabetta, never remember her, and that they surely believe her to be dead. And yet, you know how destitute she is, and almost always confined to bed with some illness or other.

I received the saddlebags with all the stuff you said you would be sending. I shared the buffalo eggs with my friends and with Signor Rondinelli. The saffron is excellent and more than enough for the pills. I have tempered four or five ounces of aloe, and I think it is very good now, having basted it with rose extract as many as seven times. With my next letter, which I shall try to write before Tuesday, I will send some of the paste I shall be making today or tomorrow, if the headache and toothache that are tormenting me will allow it. So I stop writing, but I shall continue to pray and ask God to be the one to grant you true happiness.

Most devoted daughter Sister Maria Celeste
From San Matteo. September 10, 1633.

CIX

[Sent to Siena]

Most beloved Lord and Father:

I wanted to surprise you by having Geppo appear before you all of a sudden, but I understand that Signor Geri has warned you about his arrival. I have had this idea since you arrived at Siena. Finally, the day before yesterday, I made up my mind and, at the same time, an announcement was made that all exits around the state are now open. This is as much as Signor Rondinelli tells me. He says that he did not make any mention of it in his letter because when he wrote to you the publication had not been made. I am sure you will be very pleased to see the boy, for he will give you reliable description of how we are, as well as a detailed report about your household. On our side, we will be rewarded by hearing how you are from someone who has actually seen you. In the meanwhile, think of what you might want, underwear or anything else, and let us know, because now we have a safe way of sending things.

As to the wine, which is the main subject of the letter I am answering, this very evening I will talk to Luca, our handyman, and I will ask him to look at the barrels, and take care of whatever he deems necessary. I think he is very knowledgeable in these matters.

Both Sister Luisa and I think the saffron is just perfect and, considering its quality, a bargain too, at two lire an ounce. We never had it at such good price; we usually bought it at four giuli or fifty soldi. The linen you bought at twenty crazie per pound is fine, but I don't think it is a good idea to pay that price just to make some towels and things for everyday use around the house. I gave a bundle of linen to Piera and told her to spin it very thin. We will see how it comes out. On the other hand, the linen you purchased for four giuli is marvelous. There are some nuns here who paid as much as half a scudo per pound for something as good as that. If you sent us a little more of it, we could make a beautiful fabric for wimples.

Last week, Signora Maria Tedaldi was here with her daughter, who is now a widow. She said that she would like to have you back more than ever, because now your help is needed in order to find a new husband for this young girl. She is planning to marry her off to one of the Tebaldi brothers and has no other means to get to them but you. She would be very happy if you could write and give her some advice. She asked me to tell you so, and this is what I am doing.

I am sending a good quantity of the pills coated in gold, if you want to give them away, and a roll of the others for yourself, in case you need them.

I would appreciate knowing if you like the few pastries I am sending you now. They have not come out to my full satisfaction. Every time I make things for you, my wish is that they should turn out just perfect, but that never happens. The citron morsels at the bottom of the box are probably too hard for your teeth now: they were made when you got to Siena and I had hoped to send them to you much sooner. I recommend you the box, for it is not mine.

The list of expenses is longer than usual, but I found it impossible to be more parsimonious. You will be glad to see that Geppo is doing us honor by looking so well. He had a lot of trouble recovering from his terrible illness. The seven lire that I marked down to charity were given to a very needy person on the day of the Virgin's nativity, on condition that a special prayer be said for you. If you go to the countryside with monsignor, you will find it easier to forget how far is your humble home, so try to make the best of it. And since you fret that time goes by too rapidly, as you tell me in one of your letters, these days or weeks that you must spend over there will also pass swiftly, and greater will be our happiness when we meet again.

I recommend you have the enclosed letters delivered. They are from nuns that are our friends, who, together with the abbess, Sister Arcangela, and Sister Luisa, send you affectionate greetings. And I pray our Lord God to grant you the fulfillment of all your just wishes.

Most devoted daughter Sister Maria Celeste
From San Matteo at Arcetri. September 17, 1633.

I forgot to tell you that Sister Diamante would like to know if at Siena one can find a fabric for napkins of the quality of the enclosed sample. If so, she would like you to buy a roll, and let her know the price, for her wish is to pay for it at once. The customary cost is a giulio, ten crazie or more, according the thickness of the fabric. None can be found in Florence these days.

CX

[Sent to Siena]

Most beloved Lord and Father:

I ought to have mailed you a report as soon as Giuseppe was back from Siena, and that was eight days at the first hour of the night last night. It is hard to believe that in all this time I could not manage to steal away a few moments from my duties to write a couple of lines, but this is the truth. Besides the customary routine and the responsibilities entailed by my office, which at the moment are many, Sister Luisa was taken very ill with her usual stomach trouble, so neither for me nor for her assistants was there a single moment of peace, by day or night. As I am especially beholden to Sister Luisa, I feel I must assist her without interruption. Now that she has improved a little I can breathe and also please you by letting you know that Geppo and his father arrived back here safe and sound, together with the mule, who was greatly offended for being ridden on such a long journey. I was persuaded to let the animal go by the assurances given me by those who are supposed to know better. In any case, the mule is all right now.

I was delighted to hear what the boy had to say about your condition, that you looked better than when you left, which I can easily believe, considering the comforts and the thoughtful attention of which you have been the object, first in the residence of our ambassador, then in the house of this very renowned monsignor, the archbishop. Apparently their welcome was such as to alleviate almost entirely the bitter disappointments you had to endure, and, by consequence, your health has suffered no harm. And so now, how could you fail to bless this prison of yours, and not consider very lucky a detention that has so often given you the chance to be in friendly terms with such distinguished and benign host? And, not being satisfied with paying you all the respects no one could wish greater, monsignor went to an excess of courtesy by favoring us as well, both with affectionate words and with a delicate show of consideration, for which I am sure you have thanked him on our behalf. That is all, except that I would like you to give him our regards and impress upon him that we shall exercise our gratitude for his good graces by praying for him.

As to your return, it will occur soon, if it is to be according to your hopes and our desire. For the time being, I am glad to tell you that the barrels with the red wine have been repaired. More specifically, the barrel in which the spoiled wine was stored had to be taken apart and cleaned out carefully. As for the white wine, Signor Rondinelli found three barrels in a very good state. There was one cask with some of last year's Greco in it, which filled, I believe, four or five flasks. It is a very strong wine. Some was left at the bottom, to keep the cask moist. Signor Rondinelli says that it would be enough to give them all a good washing out before the new wine is poured, but otherwise they are in good condition.

The abbess thanks you to no end for the saffron, and I for the other gifts, the linen, the hare, and the sponge-cake; the latter is really something delicious. I gave Geppo the rosary and the lippers for his cousin.

Doctor Giovanni Ronconi often comes here to see five nuns who have been in bed with a fever for quite a while now; the other day he said to me that he did not believe I had forwarded his regards to you. I told him that I had, for I have the impression I did so at least once. It is true that I was incredibly so slow-witted as to forget to return your regards to him, so, I pray you, do me the favor to remedy my oversight and write him a couple of lines. It will be easy for me to let him have your note because I am to report to him about these sick nuns every day. You must believe me when I say that not once he was here without inquiring after you and showing great concern for all you are going through.

Had I guessed your need for money, I would have sent it to you. By now you must have received the sum that Signor Alessandro[108] has forwarded to you, from what I can gather from the letter you wrote to him, which he showed to me in place of the one I ought to have received from you, and which perhaps you did not send out of pique for my not writing. You have just heard the reason for my delay. And now I say adieu and give you the good night, of which half is already gone.

Your devoted daughter Sister Maria Celeste
From San Matteo at Arcetri. October 1, 1633.

CXI

[Sent to Siena]

Most beloved Lord and Father:

I wrote you a letter on Saturday and on Sunday I received yours by the hands of Signor Gherardini. Your hope of being allowed to come back soon has given me heart to look forward to a day for which I have been longing so much. And my longing was doubled by the news that you are well, for I shall then be able to see you back in your home and in excellent health.

Be reassured that I will never stop recommending you to the Holy God with my whole being, as my concern for your bodily and spiritual well-being is much to my heart. And I will give you a proof of it. For a while now, I have been trying to see a copy of your sentence, and I have finally succeeded. Although, on the one hand, reading it has given me considerable anguish, on the other, I am glad to have seen it because I found in it a way to be of some, although limited, use to you. And that is by taking on myself the obligation that you are now under of reciting the penitential psalms once a week. I have started doing it a few days ago and I am very glad of it, because, first, that dispenses you of the duty to carry on the penance and, second, because I am persuaded that this prayer, with that glossa whereby you must promise to obey the Holy Church, will be very efficacious to you. I wish it were possible for me to take on the rest of the sentence as well, for I would gladly choose to live in a jail much narrower than the one I am living at present, if I could set you free in exchange. But we must accept things as they are and, from the many favors God has bestowed on us in the past, draw hope of receiving others in the future, as long as our faith is accompanied by good works because, as you know well, *fides sine operibus mortua est.*[109]

Dear Sister Luisa is still not well, and what with the pain and the pulling she feels on the right side from her shoulder to her thigh, she can neither rest in bed not sit up in a chair, night or day. The last time he was here, the doctor told me that, if it turns out to be a problem with a kidney, her illness will prove incurable. It wrenches my heart to see her suffer without my being able to help her at all, for no medication brings her any relief whatsoever.

Yesterday, at your house, three barrels were filled with the wine from Rose, and there is enough left to fill a keg. Signor Rondinelli was present and he was also here during the grape harvest in the orchard. He told me that the must was boiling vigorously and, although there is a small quantity—and I do not know how much—it promises to turn out very well. This is all I can quickly report for the time being. I send affectionate greetings from all of us, as usual, and may God let you prosper.

Most devoted daughter Sister Maria Celeste
From San Matteo at Arcetri. October 3, 1633.

CXII

[Sent to Siena]

Most beloved Lord and Father:

When he checked the white wine, Signor Rondinelli told me
that there were three barrels in excellent condition, and, when I
asked how long they would hold out, he said that there was no
need to warn you about them, because you surely must have seen
as much yourself. He also told me that there are other barrels
whose quality he could not guarantee. This week he was unable to
come up here, so it was impossible to continue with the inventory.
To compensate for that, I will let you in on a discovery I made,
which I think will please you. In the convent cellar there are three
or four barrels—one holding about six casks, the other five, and
the third four—which every year are filled with *verdea*,[110] but, as
this year there wasn't any *verdea*, I have sequestered them for you,
for I am sure the barrels are in good condition, with the permission to send them to your cellar for your use when you need them
and to leave them there until you will be able to do the pouring
yourself, or for the entire year, if you so decide. Let me know what
your preference is.

The San Miniato wine has not yet arrived. Of the wine loaned
out we received one barrel back from the peasants, and we poured
it into the barrel in which the bad wine was stored, the first one to
be repaired. The new wine from the orchard has not been drawn

off yet. On my request, Signor Rondinelli had a word with the blacksmith about the three casks he received; the smith promised to return them soon.

I did not forget to acknowledge the six cheeses you sent. The fault is in my language, which is none too refined and not sufficiently clear. My acknowledgment was meant to be included in the thanks I said I would like you to give monsignor the archbishop on our part, because you said the gift was coming from him. Likewise, I saw the buffalo eggs, but, hearing that they were intended for Geppo, and for his father, I left the thanks to him and said nothing.

Acknowledgments are also due for the excellent wine that monsignor sent to us, of which all the nuns had a taste, in particular Signora Giulia, who had enough for her to do some good dunking. I also thank you for the letter to be given to Signor Ronconi. I read it with great satisfaction; I sealed it and gave it to him in person yesterday morning. It was received very courteously.

I am also glad to learn that you are in good health and in excellent mood. And also that you are busy with something consonant to your liking, that is, with writing. But, for Heaven's sake, let it not be about subjects that are going to encounter the same lucky reception as those that kept you occupied in the past and about which you have already written.[111]

I wish to know if you are still enjoying the company of the archbishop, or if he left for the country, as Geppo told me he was about to do. I am convinced that this must have been of no small disappointment to you.[112]

Sister Luisa keeps to her bed, what with medicines and medical doctors, but her pains have mitigated somewhat, thank God. And God I pray to grant you his grace, and I say adieu, while returning greetings from all of us.

Your devoted daughter Sister Maria Celeste
From San Matteo at Arcetri. October 8, 1633.

At this very moment Piera tells me that the wine from our
orchard will be about one barrel and two or three flasks, and,
because it is too weak by itself, she is planning to mix it with the
wine that has just arrived. The San Miniato wine ought to be here
today, according to what Signor Niccolò's servant was saying until
yesterday. This is what I have learned just now.

CXIII

[Sent to Siena]

Most beloved Lord and Father:

The San Miniato wine is not here yet. Three days ago I wrote to Signor Geri about it. He replied that he would try to find the cause of the delay from Signor Aggiunti. I have no other news to give you because this week I haven't had the opportunity to send Geppo to Florence. He was, and still is, at San Casciano with Sir Giulio Ninci. Ninci has been ill for several days and had no one to look after him, not even to get him some food. So when he sent word to ask Sir Alessandro and me if I would let him have the boy to assist him, I could not say no. As for the canon, I shall carry out your order as soon as he sends for the money.

When Signor Gherardini was here a few days ago to pay a visit to Sister Elisabetta, who is a relative of his, he asked for me in order to give me news of you. He seems to be very devoted to you and said that he feels much reassured about you since the moment he was able to speak to you, while before he was so worried as to be quite unable to carry on his work efficiently. May it please God that the time of your return be no further off than we expected, and that you may soon enjoy the serenity of your home and the conversation of this accomplished young man. Meantime I am glad to hear how constant the archbishop is in showing you love and kindness. Nor do I fear that you will be struck out *de libro viventium*[113]—as you say—either in the world at large or in your very country. My impression, in fact, is that, though slightly diminished or shadowed by the recent turn of events, you have now been reinstated, restored, and renewed, which surprises me a lot, because I know for a fact that *nemo propheta acceptus in patria sua*[114] (I hope I have committed no barbarism in all this Latinizing). Truly, in Florence Your Lordship is loved and esteemed more than ever before. May God be praised for everything, for it is to him that we owe these favors. And I consider it my own purview to express gratitude, for I have no other wish than to be thankful, and for the great Lord to be so pleased with us as to grant you and us more blessings, and especially our eternal health and happiness in heaven.

Sister Luisa is in bed with much less pain and a little fever, but we hope they will disappear completely very soon with the help of a good medicine, which may not be as pleasing to the palate as the wine of the Siena region but, under the circumstances, more useful and necessary.

As soon as I received the six cheeses, I thought of leaving half of them for you, but I did not tell you about it because I wanted to succeed in deeds rather than in words. And indeed this cheese is so exquisite that at each meal I eat a little more of it than is my usual custom.

I sent the letter to Tordo by way of our bailiff, who learned from Tordo's wife that he is in the hospital where he is undergoing the guaiacene treatment, so it is no wonder that you received no reply from him.[115]

It has always been my wish to find out what the famous Sienese cakes are like. Now with the approach of All Saints' Day, you have the chance of letting me try some. I do not say "taste" it, because I do not wish to sound like a glutton. You have also promised, and are therefore obliged, to send the rust-colored thread I need to start making a few small things for little Galileo's Christmas present. I love the child very much, the more so because I understand from Signor Geri that he has the spirit as well as the name of his grandfather.

Sister Polissena has received an answer to that letter you had delivered to her niece. She has also received one scudo, for which she gives thanks in the enclosed note. She would like to have it delivered, and sends her regards to you, as do Mother Superior and the usual nuns.

Signor Rondinelli has not been seen for two weeks now. I am told that he is drowning in the wine of two small barrels of his, which are leaking and drive him to distraction. I told Piera to have the orchard well spaded so that the broad beans can be seeded—I should say planted—at the earliest. A laborer of Signor Niccolò Cini has arrived here just now with the letter that you wrote to his master. At the bottom of it Signor Cini has jotted down a note saying that the cost of the wine is 19 soldi per load, plus two lire for transport, which makes altogether 59 lire, and as much I gave him. To his note I added two lines of thanks.

Nothing else seems to come to mind. But I just remembered that I would like to know if Doctor Ronconi has replied to your note; if not, I will give him a good scolding next time he comes.[116] May God be always with you.

Most devoted daughter Sister Maria Celeste
From San Matteo at Arcetri. October 15, 1633.

CXIV

[Sent to Siena]

Most beloved Lord and Father:

Last Wednesday a brother of the prior of S. Firenze was here to deliver your letter and the small package with the rust-colored thread. This thread seems expensive to me, given the quality, which is rather on the thick side. The color nonetheless is very beautiful, and that makes the price of six crazie per hank acceptable.

Sister Luisa is still in bed but has improved slightly. Besides her, we have six more sisters in bed. Had this occurred at the time of the plague, we really would have been done for. One of the sick nuns is Sister Caterina Angela Anselmi, who was our abbess before the current one, a really venerable nun and a very wise woman and, after Sister Luisa, my nearest and dearest friend. Her condition is very serious, so yesterday morning she was given the sacraments and, as far as one can tell, will last a few more days. The same can be said for Sister Maria Silvia Boscoli, a young woman of twenty-two. In order to help you remember whom I am talking about, I will say that she is the one who was rumored to be the most beautiful girl in Florence for the past three hundred years. She has been in bed with uninterrupted fever for six months now, and the doctors say she is consumptive. She has become so thin that you would not recognize her. What amazes me is that, for the condition she is in, she is very vivacious and very spirited, especially when she talks. It is feared, nonetheless, that the little strength she has left, which seems to be restricted to her tongue, may suddenly vanish and abandon her poor wasted body entirely. Besides, she has little appetite and we cannot find anything she likes or, rather, anything that her stomach will hold, except a few spoonfuls of broth with some dried wild asparagus boiled in it. This season, wild asparagus is difficult to find, so I thought that perhaps some partridge soup, with that savage flavor that partridges let out, might revive her appetite a little. You write that there are plenty of partridges around Siena, so perhaps you could send a few for her, and for Sister Luisa too. As to their getting here without being damaged, there seem to be no difficulty. A few days past, our Sister Maria Maddalena Squadrini received some thrushes—that were quite fresh and in a good condition—from a brother who is the prior of the regular canons at the Monastero degli Angeli near Siena. I would be very obliged if you could find someone to bring them to us. Only the thought of it makes me feel hungry!

I am afraid that on this occasion I must be like the crow that announces only bad news, for to the above I must add that Goro, the man who worked for the Sertinis, died, leaving a family in dire circumstances. This is what I understood from his wife, who was here recently and asked me insistently to let you know about it and remind you of the promise you made to him and their daughter, Antonia, to give her a black petticoat when she got married. As she has used up the little money she had for medicines and for the funeral, the woman is now destitute and would like to know if you could help her out. I told her that I would let her know as soon as I heard from you.

I cannot adequately express all my gladness in hearing of your continued state of excellent health, except by saying that I rejoice for your well-being more than for my own. This is because I love you as much as I love myself. I also consider that if I myself were to fall ill, or if I were taken away form this world, I would scarcely care, as I am good for little or nothing at all, while as far as you are concerned, it is just the opposite, and for a variety of reasons: not only because you can be and are of service to many, but especially because you were given by God a great intellect and so much knowledge that you can serve and honor him incommensurably more than I ever could myself.

Signor Rondinelli has made an appearance again, since his wine barrels have quieted down. He returns your greetings and the same does Signor Ronconi.

I can assure you that it isn't idleness that bothers me, but rather hunger. I believe my appetite to be brought about not so much by my always being around and about, but rather by the coldness in my stomach. Perhaps it is entirely due to the fact that I never have enough time for a good sleep, for I have no time. I reckon a tonic and the papal pills will make up for it. I am saying this because I wish to be excused if this letter will seem to be put together at random, as I had to interrupt it and pick it up again more than once before reaching the end. And with this I say good-bye.

Your devoted daughter Sister Maria Celeste
From San Matteo at Arcetri. October 22, 1633.

You will find here my note to the lady ambassador that you ordered me to write in a letter I received after finishing this one. At this point I am so tired and confused that perhaps I am making no sense at all. Please read it and correct it, and also let me know if you are sending her the ivory crucifix. I hope this week you will have news concerning your return and I look forward to the announcement as much as you do.

CXV

[Sent to Siena]

Most beloved Lord and Father:

This week I decided to hold off writing to you until I could send the ortolans, but unfortunately now I am told that there are none around, that they left when the thrushes arrived. I wish I had known about this craving of yours a few weeks ago, when I was trying to think of something you might like to have. Never mind! You had no luck with the ortolans, and I have no luck with the partridges. I even caused the hawk to get lost!

Yesterday Geppo was back from San Casciano and brought those two boxes of yours—jam packed with provisions. And since you gave me absolute title to them I decided to exercise it, not by sending half of the provision to my sister-in-law, but rather by sending something, namely two puddings and some apricots to Signor Geri and telling him that he could share them with Sestilia, if he liked. I divided the rest with Signor Rondinelli, who is always so gracious and considerate toward us, and with several of my friends. It is really delicious stuff, but also very expensive, and for this reason I would not want to make another such request, to which you responded so generously. I thank you for it a hundredfold.

As to Goro's wife, I told her of your wish to come even with her and give her something when you are back. If she asks again, I will do as you tell me, and I shall proceed in the same manner with

Tordo. Ninci feels reasonably well and is very satisfied with our Geppo's assistance. Sister Luisa has begun to take a few walks from her bed. Sister Caterina died; the young nun is holding on but is always in critical condition.

The San Miniato wine has arrived. The cause of the delay seems to have been the rainy season, which was also the motive for putting off the planting of the broad beans in your orchard. They will be planted as soon as the weather improves. The lettuce and the cabbage are already in place, and there are also some onions. The artichokes are fine; there is a good quantity of lemons, but only a few oranges.

The mule has had a discharge in one eye, but now she is well again. And so is Piera, your governess, who keeps busy spinning and praying God for your speedy return. Yet I do not think her prayers are as heartfelt as mine. Even so, every time I read that you are having such a good time in Siena, I do not know what to think and what to pray for. God perhaps will reward the trust that you place in my prayers, or I should say, in a prayer that is always in my heart, for I have no time to say it aloud.

This time I will not send you any pills because I hope you will come to pick them up yourself very soon. I shall be glad to hear this week the answer that you are expecting from Rome. The comedy you sent, being penned by you, cannot be but good, though so far I have only read the first act.[117] I have many things to say, but not the time to say them, and for that reason I close. May our Lord God and the Holy Virgin be always with you. Affectionate greetings from all the usual friends.

Your devoted daughter Sister Maria Celeste
From San Matteo. Last day of October 1633.

CXVI

[Sent to Siena]

Most beloved Lord and Father:

If you could penetrate my heart and desire as you penetrate the heavens, surely you would not complain about me as you do in your last letter. You would see and be persuaded that I would love to receive your letters every day, if possible, and answer them every day, for this is the greatest pleasure I can give you and receive from you, until the time comes when God will let us enjoy each other's presence.

I think you can surmise from the disconnected way my letters are put together that I am forced to write in great haste. Last Saturday, especially, I had no time whatsoever and I could not send you my report, as I ought to have done. With your permission I can say that I am pleased that this happened, because in your present lamentation I see the excess of affection that motivates it and feel flattered. Even so, I did my duty on All Saints' Day when I gave Signor Geri a letter for you. You must have received it by now, so I will not answer all the questions that you asked in your last. I shall only say that I received the envelope for Sir Ippolito—for him nothing else arrived—and also that Geppo, after bringing the two boxes, did not go back to San Casciano, because Ninci no longer needed him. He will go to see him some time next week.

Luck answered my good prayers and led me to find the ortolans you wanted. In a few minutes I shall hand over the box, filled with flour, to Geppo, and I shall order him to go and pick the birds up at the water tank in Boboli, from one of the grand duke's hunters, whose name is Berna, or Bernino. This man is doing me a special favor by letting me have them at one lira a pair. According to Geppo, who went there to look at them yesterday, they are excellent. If I bought them from the poulterers I would have to pay as much as two giuli a pair. After they have been picked up, Signor Rondinelli will be so kind as to pack them in the box, because the boy does not have enough time to bring them up here and then take them down to town again; so he will consign them directly to Signor Geri. Enjoy them and then tell me if they have been to your satisfaction. There will be twenty ortolans in the box, just the number you wanted.

At this moment they are calling me from the infirmary, and I must stop writing. Warmest greetings, also on the part of the usual nuns, especially Sister Luisa, who is much better, thank God. May the Lord grant you true solace.

Your devoted daughter Sister Maria Celeste
From San Matteo at Arcetri. November 5, 1633.

CXVII

[Sent to Siena]

Most beloved Lord and Father:

Guccio, the innkeeper and neighbor of ours, is here on some business of his, and I take advantage of his coming in order to write you a few lines and say that in my last letter I boasted about my good luck in finding the ortolans because I thought I already had them in hand. Now I must apologize for not sending the number I expected, as you by now must have seen and heard from Signor Geri. The reason is that of the ortolans that Berna had, only eleven were in sufficiently good condition, and since Geppo made the error of taking those, I began to look for others both here and in Florence. Finally I decided to send what I had, by encouragement of the wardrobe keeper at Poggio Imperiale, who told me that in this season it is very difficult to find ortolans and that those I had were a great gift indeed. Enough: I am sure you will at least appreciate my good efforts.

Sir Ippolito sent someone to pick up the four scudi and I gave them to him. The San Miniato wine did not show up. It is impossible to dig up the orchard because the earth is too wet. The boy went to see Ninci today. Sister Luisa is better, but not quite well. She sends you warm greetings, and so do Sister Arcangela, Mother Superior, Sister Camilla, and her father, who did not come here for a long time because of the bad weather, but writes often. May our Lord keep you safe.

Your devoted daughter Sister Maria Celeste
From San Matteo. November 7, 1633.

CXVIII

[Sent to Siena]

Most beloved Lord and Father:

I write to you again to take advantage of the arrival of a man who works for Sir Santi Bindi. So I will say, first of all, that I am surprised to see that in your last letter there is no mention of any news from Rome about the decision to be made concerning your return to Florence and which we hoped would be set for All Saints' Day, as Signor Gherardini made me believe. I wish you had told me exactly how this matter is turning out, so as to have some peace of mind, and also what subject you are writing about now, if it is something I can understand and if you are not afraid I might go around telling everybody.[118]

Tordo received the four scudi, as I wrote you last Thursday, and the Bindi brothers sent their man Domenico to pick up the rent. I let them know that I will give them satisfaction as soon as you are advised of this and send your instructions. It has been impossible to work in the orchard for more than half a day so far, due to the bad weather, which I believe is also the cause of your renewed aches. The two pounds of linen you sent through Geppo seem to be of the same quality as the one you purchased for twenty crazie. It is coming out quite well, but, if we consider the price, it could be much better. On the other hand, the one pound of linen you bought for four giuli is very fine and not too expensive.

Sir Giulio Ninci is completely restored to good health, as I understand from Geppo, and sent us a few things. Sir Alessandro, his cousin, sent a citron, and with it I made the ten morsels that you find here. They are rather spicy and therefore more pleasing to the stomach than to the palate. You may try them, and if you think they are all right, offer them to monsignor, together with the rose. The pine-seed cake and the two slabs of quince tart were a gift to me from Signora Ortensia, to whom I gave in exchange one of your cakes.

I am not sending you any pills because I haven't had any time to shape them up, and besides you did not say that you need them. When the man who brings you this comes back, I will have to give him something. Let me know how much it ought to be, for I wish to be fair, but at the same time I do not want to overpay him. He comes there principally to carry out this errand.

I close with the usual recommendations, and I pray God to give you true happiness.

Your devoted daughter Sister Maria Celeste
From San Matteo at Arcetri. November 12, 1633.

The rain is still coming down in buckets and this has prevented Giovanni (this is the name of the carrier) from leaving this morning, which is Sunday. So I have time to chat a little bit longer, and let you know that, a short while ago, I had a big molar pulled out. It was totally rotten and has been giving me a lot of trouble. But the worst is that I have other teeth that will soon end up the same way. From Signor Rondinelli I learned that Vincenzo Landucci's two small children are at present been taken care by a woman who, to this purpose, has taken them to her house a few days ago. Landucci was in bed with a fever, but is recovering now.

I would like to know how often our Vincenzo wrote to you. And to answer your observation that keeping busy is good to one's health, I can say that I always thought so too; and that if too much activity does seem to me useless and hard to cope with, because at times I would rather be left alone, nonetheless I clearly see, in my sound mind, that my numerous occupations have been my deliverance. It was especially true during your long absence, God being very provident in seeing to it that I would not have a single moment of rest. This has prevented me from grieving exceedingly for you, which would have been harmful to me and a bother rather than a cause of satisfaction for you. May God be blessed, for from him I hope to receive new graces in the future, for so many he has granted us in the past. For the time being, try to be serene and confide in him, who is loyal, just, and merciful. And with this I leave you.

CXIX

[Sent to Siena]

Most beloved Lord and Father:

I received your letter, which was most welcome, together with the apricots. I gave these to Piera to distribute them to the neighbors. I was happy to read that occasionally you get out of town for a breath of fresh air, for I know how much you like the countryside and how good it is for you. May it please God that you arrive here soon to enjoy your dear home, for whose rent this morning I sent seventeen and a half scudi to the owners, who were asking for them. Here is the list of the expenses incurred for the same house.

I also want you to know that the blacksmith has returned the three barrels he owned us. His is wine from Navicello and is good enough for the servants to drink. So now all the wine that was given out, or better, that was loaned, has been returned. The *verdea* is not on the market yet, but when it is I will try to buy some of a good quality, and the man who brings you this letter will take it to you. I wanted to send you some of your oranges, but, from the samples that Piera brought to me, I could see that they are not ripe yet. If you are lucky enough to find a partridge or some such thing, I would very much like to have it for the sake of this poor girl who is dying and will only eat things from the wild. During the last full noon she was so ill that they gave her the last sacraments, but now she has picked up a bit, so we believe she will last until the next new moon. She talks in a very animated way and quite eats up her food, if we give her something tasty. Last night I was up with her all night, and, while I was feeding her, she said: "I do not believe that people who are dying eat with as much gusto as I do; but I do not care to change, and God will take care of the rest."

I pray the Lord to grant you his grace, and I send you greetings from the usual people.

Your devoted daughter Sister Maria Celeste
From San Matteo at Arcetri. November 18, 1633.

CXX

[Sent to Siena]

Most beloved Lord and Father:

Saturday night I was given your last letter and also another from the lady ambassador in Rome, which was full of thanks for the crystal and of sorrow for your not having been granted the permission to come home yet. She really seems to be as kind a lady as more than once you described her to be. I am not forwarding a letter for her because I am uncertain whether I should write or wait and see first what the verdict from Rome will be.

I will be looking for the pears you want and I certainly will find them. However, as fruit do not seem to keep at all this season, I do not know if it would be better to send the pears as soon as I can get them, or wait for you to be back, which could be a few more weeks from now, or at least my longing for it makes me fear as much.

Signor Geri gave us a share of all the fruit from his orchard. This year it wasn't as abundant and as good as expected. This I heard from Geppo, who was there to do the picking. Especially so for the pomegranates, the greater part of which was ours, but, as I said, there were only a few and rather stunted.

Next Sunday will be the beginning of Advent, so if you send the apricots, we will be very glad to eat them at supper, but the cheapest kind will be sufficient, like those you sent for the neighbors, who, says Piera, send their thanks, and she does too, and they send their regards as well. And we all do the same here and pray our Lord to favor you.

Most devoted daughter Sister Maria Celeste
From San Matteo. November 23, 1633.

Please, turn the page over.

Wednesday, late in the evening, after I had written the preceding page, Giovanni showed up with your letter. It was impossible to pass it on to Signor Geri before the following day, and this I did very early in the morning. I also received the basket with twelve thrushes. Four thrushes, which together with the others would have made up the number you gave me, must have been eaten by a nice little cat who wanted to taste them before we did, because they were not there. The cloth covering them had a big hole in it. Fortunately, the partridges and the woodcocks were at the bottom. I gave one of these and two thrushes to the sick girl who greatly appreciated them and thanks you. A partridge and also two thrushes I sent to Signor Rondinelli, and the rest we enjoyed with our friends.

I was very pleased to partake the whole lot with so many people, because things that are gotten with much diligence and toil ought to be shared by many, I think, and because the thrushes arrived rather worn out and I had to cook them in a sauce, and I was after it all day long, so that for once I gave myself entirely to the pleasure of the table.

The news that you give me about the visit here of those ladies is greatly welcome. It is the best news I can possibly have heard lately, aside from the announcement of your return. I am very attached to the ambassadress, for we are so very beholden to her, and making her personal acquaintance is what I wish more than anything else. It is true that I am rather worried about the great opinion they seem to have of me, for I am certain that I will not show in person as well as I do in my letters. You know that I am no good for small talk, or, I should say, I have no ability to carry on a conversation. I would not mind, however, to lose face in this instance—I am sure such kind people will understand—if I were able thereby to prove to that lady how much obliged I feel toward her. In the meanwhile I will be thinking what a poor nun like me could offer such a lady.

I would be grateful if you could let me have the citrons, because I do not know where to find them. I remember that Signor Aggiunti sent some beautiful ones last year. So, if you can manage to get them this year too, I will start making the morsels in my shop, for I am happy to busy myself in the service of such a distinguished monsignor, and I feel flattered to hear that he prefers these confections to any other.

Now I say good-bye again and pray for your happiness.

CXXI

[Sent to Siena]

Most beloved Lord and Father:

Last Thursday I wrote to you at length, and now I write again just to tell you that yesterday seven barrels of wine arrived from San Miniato al Tedesco. From Piera I understand that Signor Aggiunti's servant was there to supervise the filling of the barrels, and that he also paid for it, but she does not know how much exactly. One barrel, six casks worth, is filled up; another barrel up to about five casks and a half. To fill this one up, I told them to add some of the wine they are drinking now, which isn't too bad, but that they should take out several flasks of it before mixing in order to fill the barrel up to six casks. We too will take a few flasks. It is a light wine and I think you will like it in the summer, and I too enjoy it in this kind of weather. The barrel that has not been mixed will be marked and set aside, and the other will be drunk by the servants. This is all I can tell you for the time being. Now I close with the usual greetings and pray our Lord to keep you safe and sound.

Most devoted daughter Sister Maria Celeste
From San Matteo at Arcetri. November 26, 1633.

CXXII

[Sent to Siena]

Most beloved Lord and Father:

I too realize the stupidity of Giovanni, my messenger. But my wish to reach you led me to overlook everything, the more so because I received the favor of his service from the Squarcialupi mothers, who are all for me now. But that's enough.

Tordo sent someone to get the four scudi, and I gave them to him. Mother Achilla is sending back the motet. Actually, she would like to have a symphony or a ricercata,[119] and she wants you to know that the organ does not work in the high notes, because some registers are missing—I do not know which ones—so the pieces she can play are only those in the lower notes.

I want to hope, and believe it firmly too, that the ambassador, on leaving Rome, will take with him the permission for your release, and also that he will bring you here with him. I do not think I shall live to see that moment. Yet may the Lord grant it, if it is for the best.

I commend myself to you with all my love, together with the other nuns, as usual.

Your devoted daughter Sister Maria Celeste
From San Matteo at Arcetri. December 3, 1633.

CXXIII

[Sent to Siena]

Most beloved Lord and Father:

Signor Francesco Lupi, Sister Maria Vincenza's brother-in-law, was passing by before leaving for Rome, which is his city, and offered to take a letter to you or anything else I wanted to send. So I accepted his offer and I am sending this box. There are fifteen morsels in it, just as many as I was able to make with the six citrons sent by Signor Rinuccini, which were small and all damaged on one side. I think they are excellent, as far as taste goes, but as to their looks, they could be better. The weather is so wet here that I had to let them dry near the fire. I am also sending a sugar rose: you will be able to see if you would like these flowers as decorations for the basin we intend to be making on occasion of the wedding you told me about, but with smaller and prettier flowers than this one.

I received the box with the six apricots from Maestro Agostino. Thank you, in name also of those who shared them with me, who are the usual friends.

They tell me that there is a widespread rumor in Florence that you will soon be here, but, until I have it confirmed by you, I will think that this is what is being said by your dear friends, who are motivated to believe it by their love and desire to see you. For the time being, I am glad to hear about your excellent appearance, as reported to me by Maestro Agostino, who said he never saw you looking better. All must be due, not only to Holy God's help, but also to the continuous and most pleasant company of this very distinguished monsignor, the archbishop, and to the fact that now you do not wear yourself out and misbehave, as you sometimes do when you are at home. May the Lord God be thanked, and be he the one to keep you always in his grace.

Your devoted daughter Sister Maria Celeste
From San Matteo at Arcetri. December 9, 1633.

CXXIV

[Sent to Siena]

Most beloved Lord and Father:

I have received news of your return as I was picking up the pen to write to the lady ambassador and recommend this matter to her. In fact, in view of the latest postponement, I feared that you would not be able to come this year at all. So the announcement of your return came totally unexpected and I am more delighted for it. We are not the only ones to rejoice, for all these nuns, God bless them, gave demonstrations of true happiness and shared in my good fortune, just as they have often shared in my sorrows.

We greatly long to see you and are also glad that the weather is now beautiful. Signor Geri left this morning with the court for Pisa. Early in the morning I let him know at what time you will be arriving, for he knew already that you are coming; so he informed me last night. I also told him why you did not write to him, and I expressed my regrets that he could not be present at your arrival to make our happiness complete. He is so polite and thoughtful!

I am keeping the big flask with the *verdea*. Sir Francesco could not bring it to you because the trolley was already too full. You can send it to monsignor the archbishop when the litter is on its way back. I had already consigned the morsels. The casks with the white wine have been taken care of.

I cannot add anything else to this note because time is short, so we commend ourselves to you very warmly.

Your devoted daughter Sister Maria Celeste
From San Matteo. December 10, 1633.

Bibliography

SELECTED BIBLIOGRAPHY AND FURTHER READING

[Allan-Olney, Mary]. *The private Life of Galileo. Compiled principally from his correspondence and that of his eldest daughter, Sister Maria Celeste, nun in the Franciscan Convent of S. Matthew, in Arcetri*. London: Macmillan and Co., 1870. As the title indicates, this work, drawing from Favaro's *Galileo Galilei e Suor Maria Celeste*, tells the story of Galileo's family life and friendships. It contains the full texts of some of Maria Celeste's letters and extensive passages from others.

Arcangeli, Tiziana. "Hagiography" and "Theological Works." In *The Feminist Encyclopedia of Italian Literature*, edited by Rinaldina Russell, 143–145, 334-347. Westport, Conn.: Greenwood Press, 1997.

Asor Rosa, Alberto. *Galilei e la Nuova Scienza*. Bari: Laterza: 1974.

Banfi, Antonio. *Galileo e Suor Maria Celeste*. Milan: All'insegna del pesce d'oro, 1965.

Bassanese, Fiora A. "Renaissance: Letters." In *The Feminist Encyclopedia of Italian Literature*, edited by Rinaldina Russell, 290–291, Westport, Conn.: 1997.

Brooke, Rosalind B., and Christopher N. L. Brooke. "St. Clare." In *Medieval Women: Dedicated and Presented to Professor Rosalind M. T. Hill on the Occasion of Her Seventieth Birthday*, edited by Derek Baker, 275–287. Oxford: Basil Blackwell for the Ecclesiastical History Society, 1978.

Bolton, Brenda M. "Mulieres Sanctae." In *Women in Medieval Society*. Edited by Susan Mosher Stuard, 141–158. Philadelphia: University of Pennsylvania Press, 1976.

Bulferetti, Luigi. *Galileo Galilei nella società del suo tempo*. Manduria (Taranto): Lacaita, 1973.

Calvi, Giulia. "Una metafora degli scambi sociali: la peste fiorentina del 1630." *Quaderni storici* 56 (1984): 35–64.

Canepa Nancy L. "The Writing behind the Wall: Arcangela Tarabotti's *Inferno monacale* and Cloistered Autobiography in the Seventeenth Century." *Forum Italicum* 3, no. 1 (1996): 1–23.

Canosa, Romano. *Il velo e il cappuccio: monacazioni forzate e sessualità nei conventi femminili in Italia tra Quattrocento e Settecento*. Rome: Sapere 2000, 1991.

Cantù, Cesare. *Racconti storici e morali*. Milan: Libreria Paolo Carrara, 1871, 61–92.

Cocco, Mia. "Alessandra Macinghi Strozzi." In *Italian Women Writers: A Bio-Bibliographical Sourcebook*, edited by Rinaldina Russell, 198–206. Westport, Conn.: Greenwood Press, 1994.

Cochrane, Eric. *Tradition and Enlightenment in the Tuscan Academies, 1690–1800*. Rome: Tradizioni di storia e letteratura, 1961.

Coyne, G. V. ed. *The Galileo Affair, A Meeting of Faith and Science: Proceedings of the Cracow Conference, May 24–27, 1984*. Città del Vaticano: Specola Vaticana, 1985.

Doglio, Maria Luisa. *Lettera e donna. Scrittura epistolare al femminile tra Quattro e Cinquecento*. Roma: Bulzoni, 1993.

Drake, Stillman, *Discoveries and Opinions of Galileo*. Translated with an introduction and notes by Stillman Drake. New York: Doubleday, 1957.

———"Galileo: Abiographical sketch." In *Galileo Man of Science,* edited by Ernan McMullin, 52–66. New York: Basic Books, 1967.

———*Galileo Pioneer Scientist*. Toronto: Toronto University Press, 1990.

Evangelisti, Silvia. "Memoria di antiche madri. I generi della storiografia monastica femminile in Italia (secc. XV–XVIII)." In *La voz del silencio. Fuentes directas para la historia de las mujeres, siglos III al CVI*, edited by C. Segura, 221–249. Madrid: Association Cultural Al-Mundayua, 1992.

Fantoli, Annibale. *Galileo for Copernicanism and for the Church*. Rome: Vatican Observatory Foundation, 1994.

Favaro, Antonio. *Documenti inediti sulla primogenita di Galileo*. Padova: Tipografia del Seminario, 1881.

———*Galileo Galilei e lo Studio di Padova*. Vol. 2. Florence: Le Monnier, 1883. For Virginia Galilei see pp. 63, 203–204, 304, 310.

———*Amici e corrispondenti di Galileo*. Vols. 1–3. Firenze: Libreria Editrice Salimbeni, 1983.

Ferrero, Giuseppe Guido. "Introduzione." In *Lettere del Cinquecento*, edited by G. G. Ferrero, 9–26. Torino: UTET, 1967.

Finocchiaro, Maurice A. ed. and trans. *Galileo on the World Systems. A New Abridged Translation and Guide*. Berkeley: University of California Press, 1997.

Franco, Veronica. *Lettere,* edited by Stefano Bianchi. Rome: Salerno Editrice, 1998.

Galilei, Galileo. *Opere.* National edition edited by A. Favaro, I. del Lungo, and U. Marchesini. Vols. 1–20. Florence: Barbèra, 1890–1809.

——*Dialogue Concerning the Two Chief World Systems.* Edited and translated by Stillman Drake. Berkeley: University of California Press, 1967.

——*Two New Sciences.* Edited and translated by Stillman Drake. Madison: University of Wisconsin Press, 1974.

Gebler, Karl von. *Galileo Galilei and the Roman Curia.* Merrick, N. Y: McGraw-Hill, 1965.

Gymonat, Ludovico. *Galileo Galilei: A biography and inquiry into his philosophy of science.* Foreward by Giorgio de Santillana. Translated with additional notes and appendix by Stillman Drake. New York: MacGraw-Hill, 1957.

King, Margaret L., *Women of the Renaissance.* Chicago: The University of Chicago Press, 1991.

King, Margaret L. and Albert Rabil, Jr., eds. *Her Immaculate Hand. Selected Works by and About The Women Humanists of Quattrocento Italy.* Binghamton, N. Y: Medieval & Renaissance Texts and Studies, 1983.

Kirshner, Julius, and Anthony Molho. "The Dowry Fund and the Marriage Market in Early Quattrocento Florence." *Journal of Modern History* 50 (1978): 403–438.

Klapisch-Zuber, Christiane. "Le chiavi fiorentine di Barbablù: l'apprendimento della lettura a Firenze nel XV secolo." *Quaderni storici* 19, no. 3 (1984): 765–792.

Macinghi Strozzi, Alessandra. *Tempo di affetti e di mercanti. Lettere ai figli esuli,* edited by Angela Bianchini. Milan: Garzanti, 1987.

Mazzoni, Cristina. "Mysticism." In *The Feminist Encyclopedia of Italian Literature,* edited by Rinaldina Russell, 216–218. Wesport, Conn.: Greenwood Press, 1997.

Nelli, Batista Clemente de'. *Vita e commercio letterario di Galileo Galilei.* 2 vols. Losanne, 1793.

Noffke, Suzanne. "Caterina da Siena." In *Italian Women Writers: A Bio-Bibliographical Sourcebook,* edited by Rinaldina Russell, 58–66. Wesport, Conn.: Greenwood Press, 1994.

Pezzarossa, F. "'Non mi peserà la penna.' A proposito di alcuni contributi su scrittura e mondo femminile nel Quattrocento fiorentino." *Lettere italiane* 41 (1989): 250–260.

Politi, Alessandro P. *Vita della serva di Dio Suor Maria Angiola monaca professa nel monastero di San Matteo in Arcetri.* Florence: P. G. Viviani, 1738.

Rabil, Albert, Jr. *Laura Cereta: A Quattrocento Humanist.* Binghamton, N.Y.: Medieval and Renaissance Texts and Studies, 1981.

——"Laura Cereta." In *Italian Women Writers: A Bio-Bibliographical Sourcebook,* edited by Rinaldina Russell, 67–75. Westport, Connecticut-London: Greenwood Press, 1994.

Robin, Diana. *The Renaissance Feminism and the Humanism of Laura Cereta.* Chicago: University of Chicago Press, 1996.

——"Humanism." In *The Feminist Encyclopedia of Italian Literature,* edited by Rinaldina Russell, 153–157. Westport, Conn.: Greenwood Press, 1997.

Rosenthal, Margaret. "A Courtesan's Voice: Epistolary Self-Portraiture in Veronica Franco's *Terze Rime*." In *Writing the Female Voice: Essays on Epistolary Literature*, edited by Elisabeth Goldsmith, 3–24. Boston: Northeastern University Press, 1999.

Roston, James, Jr. *Galileo. A Life*. New York: Harper Collins, 1994.

Russell, Rinaldina. "Celeste Galilei." In *An Encyclopedia of Continental Women Writers*, edited by Katharina M. Wilson, 348–349. Vol. 1. New York: Garland Publishing, 1991.

Santillana, Giorgio de. *The Crime of Galileo Galilei*. Chicago: The University of Chicago Press, 1955.

Sobel, Dava. *Galileo's Daughter*. New York: Walker, 1999.

Tornabuoni, Lucrezia. *Lettere*. Edited by Patrizia Salvadori. Florence: Olschki, 1993.

Trexler, Richard C. "Le Célibat à la fin du Moyen Age: les réligieuses de Florence." *Annales: Economies-Sociétés-Civilisations* 27 (1972): 1329-1350.

Wallace William S. *Reinterpreting Galileo*. Princeton, N. J.: Princeton University Press, 1984.

Weaver, Elissa B. "Spiritual Fun: A Study of Sixteenth-Century Tuscan Convent Theater." In *Women in the Middle Ages and the Renaissance: Literary and Historical Perspectives*, edited by Mary Beth Rose, 173–206. Syracuse, N. Y.: Syracuse University Press, 1989.

——"Arcangela Tarabotti." In *Italian Women Writers: A Bio-Bibliographical Sourcebook*, edited by Rinaldina Russell, 414–422. Westport-Conn.: Greenwood Press, 1994.

——"Nun." In *The Feminist Encyclopedia of Italian Literature*, edited by Rinaldina Russell, 236–238. Westport, Conn.: Greenwood Press, 1994.

Westfall, Richard S. *Essays on the Trial of Galileo.* Notre Dame, Ind.: University of Notre Dame Press, 1989.

Zarri, Gabriella. "Monasteri femminili e città (secoli XV–XVII). In *Storia d'Italia. Annali 9: La Chiesa e il potere politico dal Medioevo all'età contemporane,* edited by Giorgio Chittolini and Giovanna Miccoli, 359–429. Turin: Einaudi, 1986.

EDITIONS OF SISTER MARIA CELESTE'S LETTERS

Albèri, Eugenio, ed. *Le opere di Galileo Galilei.* Vol. 9. Florence, 1852. It contains twenty-seven letters on pp, 29, 32–34, 46, 57, 96, 111, 138, 149, 155, 194, 207, 216, 224, 226, 248, 250, 333, 346, 351, 366, 369, 400, 404, 409.

[Allan-Olney, Mary]. *The private Life of Galileo. Compiled principally from his correspondence and that of his eldest daughter, Sister Maria Celeste, nun in the Franciscan Convent of S. Matthew, in Arcetri.* London: Macmillan and Co., 1870. It contains numerous letters and excerpts, as they are needed to tell the story of Galileo and Maria Celeste.

Arduini, Carlo. *La primogenita di Galileo Galilei rivelata dalle sue lettere edite e inedite.* Florence: Le Monnier, 1864. It contains 121 letters, some in a mangled form.

Favaro, Carlo. *Galileo Galilei e Suor Maria Celeste.* Florence: Barbèra, 1891. This is the first complete edition and was reissued in 1935.

Galilei, Celeste. *Lettere al padre.* Genova: ECIG, 1992.

Saverio Francesco, and Maria Rossi. *Galileo Galilei nelle lettere della figlia Suor Maria Celeste.* Lanciano: Carabba, 1984.

Venturi, Gianbattista. *Memorie e lettere inedite finora o disperse di Galileo Galilei.* Vol. 1. Modena: G. Vincenzio, 1821. It contains a few excerpts on pp. 222–224.

Notes

1. At the time of my writing this introduction, Darva Sobel's volume on Galileo's daughter, which I have placed in the bibliography, had not come out. In fact, it was the announcement of the imminent publication of that book that induced the publisher I had first chosen for my translation to return my manuscript.

2. Virginia, Galileo's favorite sibling, had been buried the previous day. In 1591 she married Benedetto Landucci, whose father, Luca, had been the Florentine ambassador to Rome at the time of Pope Leo X. In Virginia's marriage contract, Galileo promised to pay the groom a dowry that in view of his precarious financial situation, can only be called extravagant. Being unable either to disburse the sum or to pay regular installments, he kept a not too friendly relationship with his brother-in-law, who in 1605 went as far as to threaten Galileo with imprisonment.

3. This is Villa Segni, later Villa "Ibizzi, which Galileo rented at Bellosguardo, in the outskirts of Florence. Next to it, and behind the Piazzale Michelangelo, rises the hill of Arcetri.

4. Urban VIII was Maffeo Barberini (1568–1644), who, when a cardinal, had been sympathetic to Galileo's views. This led the scientist to believe that the 1616

injunction by the church to abandon the Copernican theory could be safely disregarded.

5. The date is incomplete here, as is incomplete or missing in several of the following letters. When a date can be inferred from a topic discussed by Maria Celeste, I have placed it in parentheses.

6. It seems that Galileo intermittently suffered from arthritic and rheumatic fevers.

7. Sister Chiara was the daughter of Benedetto Landucci and Virginia Galilei. See note 2.

8. Benedetto Landucci. See notes 2 and 7.

9. This was the abbess of the convent. Sister Maria Celeste refers to the incumbent abbess as "mother," "mother superior," or "mother the abbess." In general, older nuns were addressed as "mothers," while young ones were called "sisters."

10. Galileo had a way of procuring a special type of thread from Brescia for both his daughter and the grand duchess.

11. Galileo's servant.

12. It probably refers to the conventual regulations against having guests at the nuns' table.

13. Galileo will not leave for Rome until April 24 of the following year. See letter XIV.

14. We do not know what was Vincenzo's "error" at this time, but from his father's correspondence we can infer that this was not the only one he made in his student years. See Favaro 1935, 135–136.

15. This was *The Assayer (Il saggiatore)*, published that very day, November 21, 1623.

16. Sister Maria Celeste distinguishes between religious orders and secular clergy.

17. At the end of this memo, Galileo wrote: "Sister Maria Celeste writes to Rome."

18. Galileo went to Rome on April 24, 1624, to pay homage to the new pontiff and remained there until June of the same year. Urban VIII received him warmly, promised a subsidy for his son, Vincenzo, but was equivocal in regard to the Copernican system. In the fall of the same year Galileo began to write the *Dialogue*, where he discussed the heliocentric theory, thus disregarding the written promise made to the Holy Office in 1616.

19. In 1603 Federico Cesi, marquis and later prince of Monticelli, son of the duke of Aquasparta, founded the Accademia dei Lincei, a society dedicated to philosophy and science (today the National Italian Academy of Sciences). Galileo had been made a member in 1611.

20. Virginio Cesarini, a duke and nephew of Prince Cesi, was a member of the Accademia dei Lincei and was Lord Chamberlain to Pope Urban VIII. *The Assayer* was written in the form of a letter to him. He was thirty years of age when he died.

21. I place in brackets all presumptive dates, as indicated by A. Favaro in *Galileo Galilei e suor Maria Celeste*. Florence: Barbèra, 1935.

22. Galileo was free because the court had temporarily moved to Pisa, as it often did.

23. For this and a few more letters, Sister Maria Celeste set the date *ab incarnatione.* In order to preserve the chronological continuity of the text, I give dates according to our calendar.

24. These were the children of Galileo's brother, Michelangelo, who, with their mother, lived with Galileo from 1627 to 1628. Michelangelo remained in Munich, where he was instrumentalist in the court chapel choir and the not too well compensated music master of the elector of Bavaria, Maximilian of Wittelsbach. I translate *mostaccioli* as "aniseed cakes," for they are made with bread dough mixed with must and aniseed and sometimes sprinkled on top with pine-seeds or raisins.

25. When he fell ill, Galileo had himself taken to the house of this Signora Barbara in Florence, leaving his sister-in-law and her children at Bellosguardo. It may be surmised that the quiet atmosphere and proximity of medical care were the reasons for his move; but Anna Chiara and her husband added Galileo's decamping to their long list of grievances. In his letter to his brother, dated March 24, 1628, Michelangelo insinuated that Galileo's move to Florence showed that he could dispose of "individuals" more apt to his needs than Anna Chiara was.

26. This is either Signora Barbara's address or Galileo's mail deposit in Florence. See note 25.

27. Believing that he was about to die, Galileo had called his son from Pisa, where he attended the university.

28. Little Alberto, or Albertino, was one of Michelangelo's children. Many years later, Alberto began working at the Medici court.

29. See note 25.

30. Mechilde was Michelangelo's eldest daughter, who had remained in Munich to take care of her father.

31. Flaminio Papazzoni's stinginess—Favaro infers—had become proverbial in Galileo's family.

32. Several coins are mentioned throughout the letters: besides the scudo, which was a gold coin, there was the giulio, made of silver; the crazia, made of silver and copper; the piastra, of the same value as the scudo, and smaller denominations such as soldo and quattrino.

33. These are *biscotti,* nowadays found on the menu in most Florentine restaurants, where they are served with *vin santo.*

34. An old nun.

35. At this time, Galileo was writing the *Dialogue on the Two Chief Systems of the World.* He had started working on this famous book in 1624, interrupted his writing in 1626 to pursue some studies on magnetism, and picked it up again in the fall of 1628.

36. The marriage contract was signed at the end of 1628. Earlier that year Vincenzo had taken his law degree at the University of Pisa and was twenty-three when, on January 29, 1629, he married Sestilia, daughter of Carlo Bocchineri of Prato. Of Sestilia's three brothers, all working in the ducal bureaucracy, Geri is the one often mentioned in these letters. After Sister Maria Celeste's death, Galileo fell in love with Sestilia's older sister, Alessandra, his junior of thirty years. She had returned with her third husband from the court of Vienna, where she had been lady-in-waiting of Eleonora Gonzaga, wife of the Emperor Ferdinand.

37. Ancient string instrument resembling the lute.

38. This was a girl for whose board at the convent of San Matteo Galileo had been paying.

39. Galileo's housekeeper.

40. At this time Sestilia was pregnant.

41. This was the eighty-year-old nun and Sister Luisa's teacher. See letter XLI.

42. The convent's doorkeeper.

43. "Sweetmeat" translates from *zibaldone,* today called *zabardone.* It is a mixture of candied fruit, pine-seed, and raisins, flavored with nut-meg and cinnamon.

44. See note 33.

45. Galileo was planning to go to Rome to solicit the authorities' permission to print the *Dialogue,* which he was then completing.

46. Galileo left for Rome with the manuscript of the *Dialogue* on May 1, 1630, and arrived there on May 3. He stayed at the residence of the Florentine ambassador, Francesco Niccolini. This is the only extant letter sent to Rome on the occasion of this trip.

47. Caterina Riccardi was the wife of the Florentine ambassador, Francesco Niccolini, and sister of Niccolò Riccardi, Master of the Sacred Palace, who was in charge of permissions to print.

48. Galileo is back in his villa at Bellosguardo. He had left Rome on May 26, with the reassurance that the *Dialogue* could be printed on the condition he made some revisions following the instructions of the Holy Office.

49. This was the daughter of Vincenzo Landucci, son of Virginia Galilei Landucci and Galileo's niece. The frequent occurrence of the name Vincenzo in Galileo's extended family was a homage to his father, Vincenzo Galilei (c.1520–1591), musicologist, composer and member of

Camerata fiorentina, a group of literati, composers, and musical theorists who brought about the birth of opera.

50. Ferdinando II had succeeded his father, Cosimo II, in 1622—he was then eleven years old—under the joint regency of his mother, Maria Magdalena of Austria, and his grandmother, Maria Christina of Lorraine. He assumed the direction of the grand duchy in 1628, when he was eighteen.

51. This is Sister Maria Celeste's first reference to the plague. It broke out in this part of Italy in the summer of 1630, decreased in the first months of the following year, and picked up again in the spring of 1633. In Florence, and in the countryside one mile around it, the death toll was almost fourteen thousand. The information is given by Francesco Rondinelli—often mentioned in these letters—in the preface of his *Relazione del contagio stato in Firenze l'anno 1630 e 1633*. (Florence: G. B. Baldini, 1634). In the territories of Lombardy, Venice, Piedmont, and Romagna, the mortality is estimated to have been of one million. Brought into Italy by the German troops of the Imperial army who laid siege to Mantova in 1630, the pestilence is described by Alessandro Manzoni in *The Betrothed*.

52. Fearing the contagion, Vincenzo ran away from Florence to a villa near Prato belonging to the Bocchineri family, leaving his little son in Galileo's care.

53. A reference to *linceo* and to Accademia dei Lincei (academy of the lynx-eyed men), of which Galileo was a member. See note 19.

54. The ingratitude Sister Maria Celeste refers to here must have been that of Galileo's brother, Michelangelo. Galileo, however, had other difficulties to worry about at this time.

With Federico Cesi's death in August, he lost a powerful supporter and the publisher of the *Dialogue*. As a consequence, he sought permission to publish in Florence, where he now had more powerful protectors, but the injunction to write a new introduction and conclusion remained, and the ecclesiastical fiat from Rome was slow to come.

55. Galileo had loaned Ninci a considerable sum of money. See *Spigolature Galileiane dalla Autografoteca Campori in Modena,* ed. Antonio Favaro (Modena, 1882), 16.

56. An electuary is a medicine composed of drugs mixed with honey.

57. Rondinelli tells us that the most popular antidote for the plague was prepared with a recipe going all the way back to Roman times. Its ingredients were dried figs, nuts, rue, honey, and salt *(Relazione del contagio,* 34).

58. "Telescope" translates from *occhiale,* which is the word Galileo used to indicate that instrument. Favaro thought that Sister Maria Celeste could not have asked for the telescope, but that she rather asked for the microscope, which, however, Galileo called *occhialino.*

59. Piera was Galileo's new housekeeper. We will hear a lot about her in the following letters.

60. These are the dowries due to the convent on the day the novices took the veil and became nuns.

61. Silence was enforced during the period of partial fasting, which in Franciscan monasteries preceded Christmas.

62. Being winter, it must have been after midnight.

63. Galileo was busy writing the revisions to the *Dialogue* suggested by the Holy Office during his trip to Rome. He had been instructed to write a new preface and a conclusion

that clearly presented the Copernican theory as a simple mathematical hypothesis.

64. Michelangelo Galilei died in Munich on January 3, 1631.

65. Ancient medicinal mixture made with vinegar and honey.

66. Galileo followed up this matter: at the end of this page he wrote the name of the man who was suing Signora Landi.

67. I have not been able to ascertain whether this Rinuccini was a relative of the poet Ottavio Rinuccini, author of *Dafne* and *Arianna,* and a member of the Camerata fiorentina. See note 49.

68. These were called "papal pills" probably because they were of a very good quality.

69. A mineral water with therapeutic properties, from Tettuccio.

70. Only the month is indicated at the foot of this letter. In July, Father Niccolò Riccardi of the Sacred College sent a preface for Galileo's *Dialogue* to the Inquisitor in Florence, with the instruction that the author could edit it but not change its meaning and that the argument in support of the Copernican theory, that is, Galileo's theory of the tides, ought not be mentioned in the book.

71. There is a time gap between this letter dated August 30, 1631, and the next, dated February 5, 1633. At the end of the summer of 1631, Galileo moved to Arcetri, into a villa adjacent to the convent, and the correspondence with his daughter is interrupted. The next letter is the first one Sister Maria Celeste sent to her father while he was traveling toward Rome in the winter of 1633.

72. After much procrastination, Galileo left Arcetri on January 11, 1633. Much had occurred in the meanwhile. In February 20, 1632, the *Dialogue* had come out of the

Florentine presses, and the author immediately distributed thirty-two copies to members of the scientific community in Italy and abroad. It seems that Pope Urban VIII saw the book only in August, and soon after he ordered to suspend all sales. In October of the same year, Galileo was told to report to the commissary general of the Holy Office in Rome, but he delayed his departure several times with the excuse of poor health.

73. Because of the plague spreading in Tuscany, Galileo and his party were obliged to stop for twenty days as a precautionary measure at Ponte Centina, on the border between Tuscany and the pontifical states.

74. Galileo had invited Francesco Rondinelli to stay at Il Gioiello, the house newly rented near the convent of San Matteo. Rondinelli was the librarian of Grand Duke Ferdinando II and the author of a very detailed report on the Florentine epidemic of 1630–1633. See notes 51 and 86.

75. Giuseppe, often called Geppo and more often "the boy" in the Italian text, was a young servant of Galileo.

76. Galileo arrived in Rome on February 13 and was immediately ordered not to leave the premises of the Florentine ambassador's palace, now Villa Medici.

77. This is Vincenzo Landucci, the son of Galileo's sister Virginia and Benedetto Landucci. See notes 2 and 7.

78. See note 75.

79. Mario Guiducci was a pupil and follower of Galileo. In 1618, when Father Orazio Grassi, mathematician at the Roman College, delivered a public lecture on comets, Guiducci presented a paper at the Florentine Academy, advancing Galileo's ideas on the same subject and criti-

cizing the theory advanced by Grassi. Guiducci's *Speech on the Comets* was published the following year and, according to Galileo's acolytes, marked the beginning of his disfavor with the scientists of the Collegio Romano.

80. On the contrary, at this time, the Holy Office was setting up Galileo's trial and was to arraign him around the middle of April. There was never any question that the Roman authorities would accept the Copernican system. The legal premise of Galileo's trial and condemnation was his disobedience to church orders not to discuss the Copernican view. Galileo defended himself by maintaining that the injunction was about upholding that theory, not discussing it per se.

81. An assistant of Galileo.

82. Galileo might have sent reassuring news to Florence, but, in fact, things were not looking up and Ambassador Niccolini, who had a direct line to the Holy Office, was trying to persuade him to plead guilty.

83. Benedetto Castelli was a former student of Galileo and is considered to have been his best. By this time, he was an expert on hydrodynamics and a professor of mathematics at the University of Pisa.

84. Anna Maria Vajani was a painter whom Galileo had met on a previous trip to Rome.

85. At this time Galileo was being interrogated by the judges of the Holy Office and was detained in its prisons. During his detention, Signora Niccolini will take upon herself the task of writing to Sister Maria Celeste. See letter LXXXVI.

86. The symptoms described by Sister Maria Celeste correspond to the three forms taken by the epidemic, according to pp. 27 and 171–172 of Francesco Rondinelli's

report (see note 51). Some victims developed high fever, together with bubonic swellings in the groins, armpits, or, at times, behind the ears or with carbuncles on several parts of their bodies. These were the signs of the bubonic plague. The victims of the septicemic plague developed a cutaneous hemorrhage, which gave way to livid patches. Those affected by the pneumatic form of the disease contracted lung infection. All the sick suffered from severe thirst, headache, vomit, and, at times, delirium. It will be noticed that there were no victims in San Matteo. Rondinelli writes that Florentine convents suffered few casualties, thanks to their isolation and to the special restrictions that the religious authorities imposed on them at the time of the plague. Archbishop Bardi ruled that no one should enter the convents, with the sole exception of doctors and confessors, and that four nuns should keep guard at the entrance at all times, thoroughly checking what was introduced into the premises and handling with forceps everything possible and/or washing it in vinegar. The nuns themselves were required to go and pick fruits and vegetables directly from the fields, and buy what was needed from the shops early in the day before the merchandise was handled by the public; they also had to mill the convent's wheat and carry the sacks to the convent without letting come into contact with outsiders (Rondinelli, 31).

87. Galileo wrote about his detention in the prison of the Holy Office in his letter of April 16 to Geri Bocchineri.

88. There was a recrudescence of the plague in the spring of 1633. See Giulia Calvi, "Una metafora degli scambi sociali:

la peste fiorentina del 1630." *Quaderni storici* 56 (1984): 35–64.

89. It should be noticed that concerned about the possible damage done to his prestige in Florence, especially at the court of the young grand duke and his devout mother and grandmother, Galileo kept sending reassuring letters to his friends and followers in which he described his situation in more optimistic terms that his case warranted.

90. For the rent of Galileo's house, Il Gioiello, whose ownership had passed from Esaù Martellini to Ginevra Martellini Bini.

91. Impruneta was then a village a few miles from Florence. It was not unusual to turn to the divinity when all other measures against the plague had failed.

92. The procession went by the house on the Costa (behind and above Palazzo Pitti), which was owned by Galileo and occupied by his son, Vincenzo, and two of the Bocchineri brothers. Later Geri Bocchineri wrote to Galileo that in honor of the Virgin—and according to the custom in such circumstances—the Bocchineri brothers set up a decoration in front of the house so elaborate and ingenious—it contained a spouting fountain among other things—that people believed that Galileo had something to do with it.

93. There seems to be no logic in the cause-effect sequence that Sister Maria Celeste is presenting. In fact, the well-to-do people left the city and withdrew into their villas so as to avoid the contagion. Francesco Rondinelli tells us that only twenty-five members of the nobility died in Florence. *Relazione del contagio*, 34.

94. This was of course a most distressing time for Galileo, and his drinking is a reflection of it.

95. See letter LXXX.

96. In any city, a *lazzaretto* was the quarantine hospital where the health officials confined the plague-stricken people who could not be cared for at home.

97. Sister Maria Celeste erroneously believed that her father was free to leave Rome, while, in fact, his most harrowing time in that city was yet to come.

98. This Arcangela was a Landucci.

99. The plague-stricken people who did not want to be taken to the *lazzaretto* were quarantined in their homes.

100. When the news of the accusations leveled at Galileo arrived in Florence, Geri Bocchineri and Niccolò Aggiunti—the latter a pupil and acolyte of the scientist—went to Il Gioiello and retrieved some compromising documents.

101. Being summer, it must have been between after 11 P.M.

102. For Mario Guiducci see note 79.

103. Sister Maria Celeste calls this exchange "wine for wine." It consisted in giving a certain party a quantity of wine that would not keep for long, and later receiving from the same party the same quantity of a newer wine in exchange.

104. Being summer, it must have been about 11 PM. See notes 62 and 101.

105. Parenti's will, dated August 24, 1633, can be seen in the Archivio Notarile of Florence, in the register 14722, 7: 10. It belonged to Vincenzo Vespignani, attorney.

106. The moggio (plural: moggia) was a measure of capacity varying at different times and in different places.

107. The "buffalo eggs" were a mozzarella cheese made with buffalo milk.

108. Alessandro Ninci was the parish priest of Santa Maria a Campoli and had some business dealings with Galileo. It may be assumed that Alessandro had pledged to return the money due by his deceased brother. See letter LIII.

109. Faith without works is dead. This was the basic principle of Counter Reformation doctrine: faith with good works, not faith alone as the Protestants believe, will save humankind.

110. A type of white wine. The *verdea* produced at Arcetri was renowned.

111. As soon as he arrived in Siena, Galileo began writing *Discourses and Mathematical Demonstrations about Two New Sciences Belonging to Mechanics and Local Motions.* The book is considered to represent the foundation of classical mechanics.

112. Galileo was not allowed to accompany his host on the planned trip to the countryside. Precise instructions arrived from the Holy Office that he was not to move from the archiepiscopal palace.

113. From the book of the living.

114. Nobody is a prophet in his own country.

115. Tordo was the nickname of Ippolito Mariani, the technician to whom Galileo, on becoming progressively blind around 1637, will contract the manufacture of his telescope.

116. Doctor Ronconi's note can be found among Galileo's papers.

117. This comedy has not come down to us. Among Galileo's papers there is the sketch of a play that is too licentious to have been planned for a convent performance.

118. See letter CXII. In his new book, *Two New Sciences,* Galileo set aside the Copernican theory and went on to

make a systematic presentation of his extensive research on dynamics. The volume was published in Leiden, Holland, in 1638 and was not condemned by the church. See note 111.

119. In the seventeenth century, the symphony was the instrumental introduction to an opera or oratorio. The ricercata was a composition similar to the toccata.

About the Author

Rinaldina Russell is a professor of Italian literature at Queens College, CUNY. She has published books and articles on medieval and renaissance poetry, has edited *Italian Women Writers* (1994), *A Feminist Encyclopedia of Italian Literature* (1997), and has co-translated Tullia d'Aragona's *Dialogue on the Infinity of Love* (1997).

Printed in the United States
3292